Floral Splendor

A Coloring Adventure

Creative Quill Press

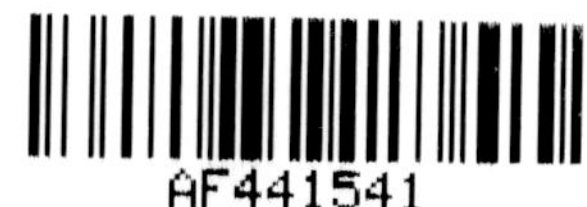

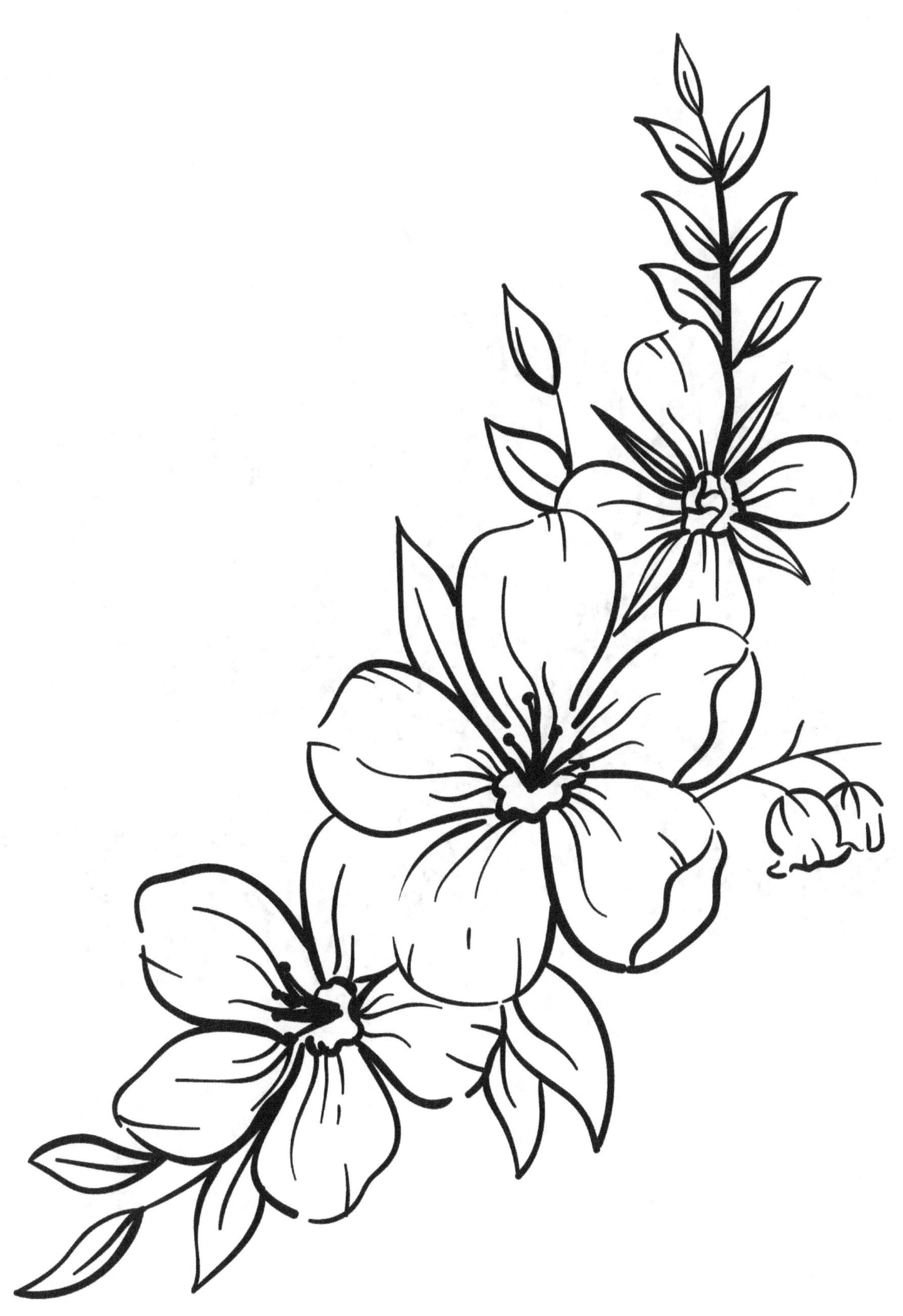

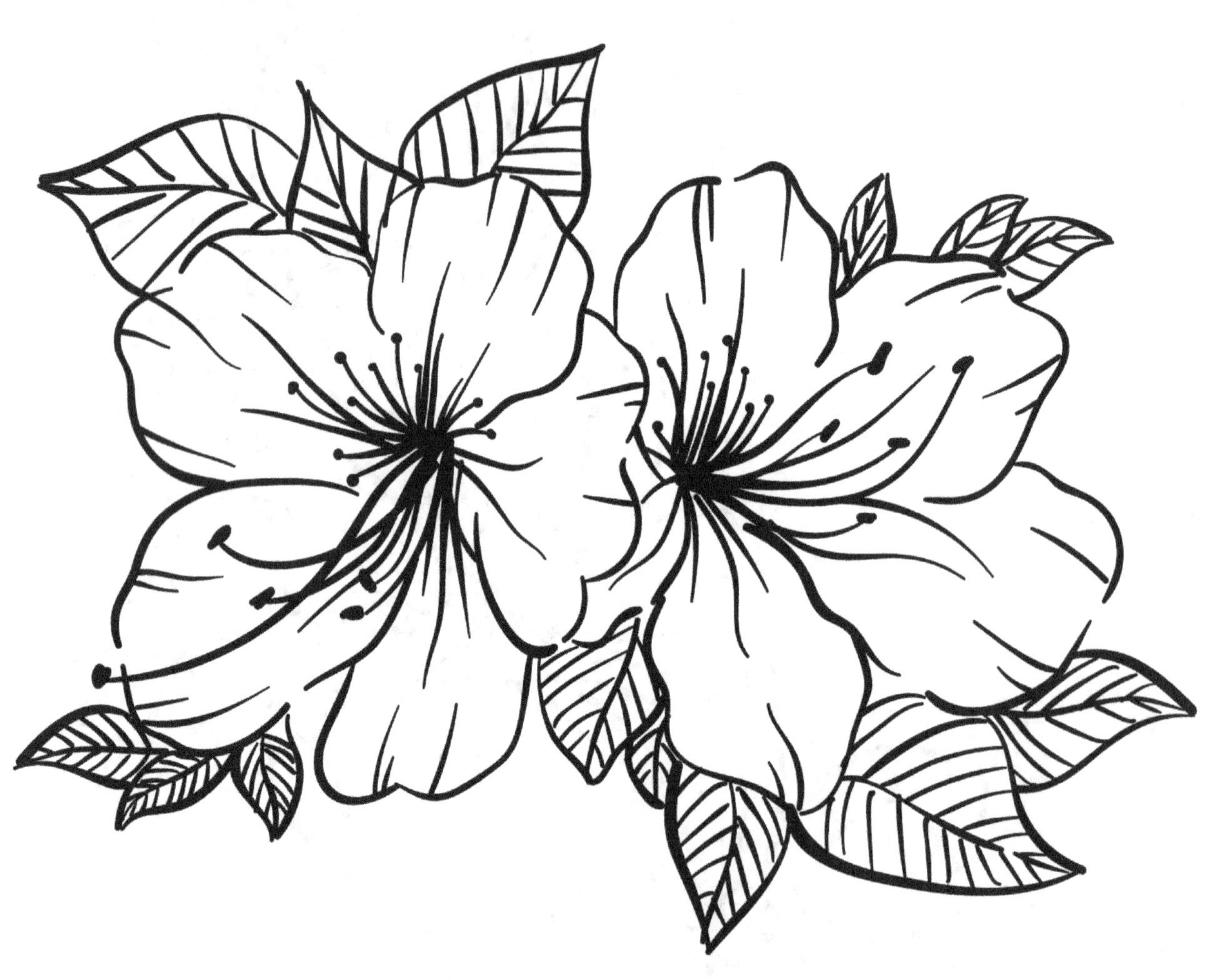

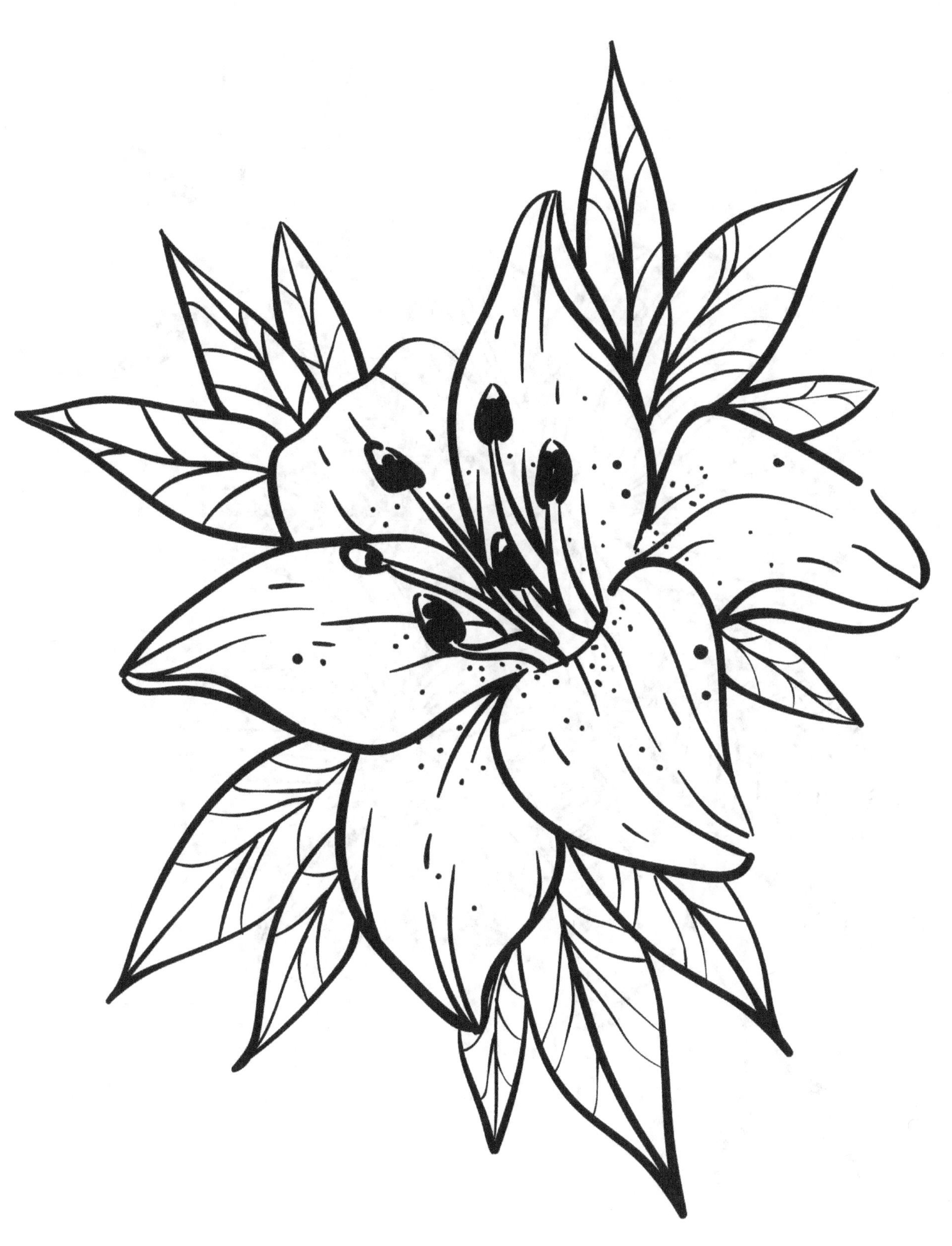

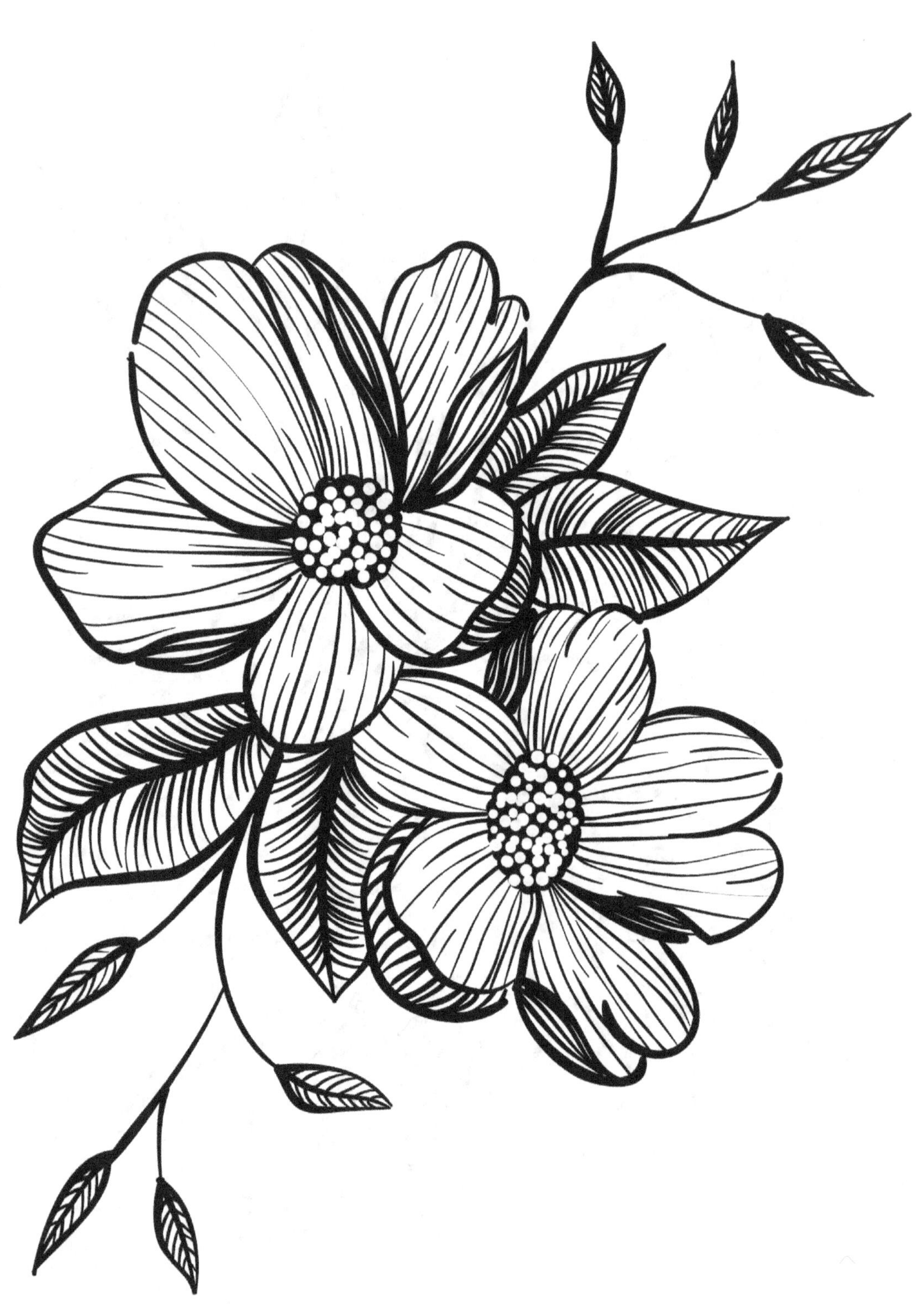

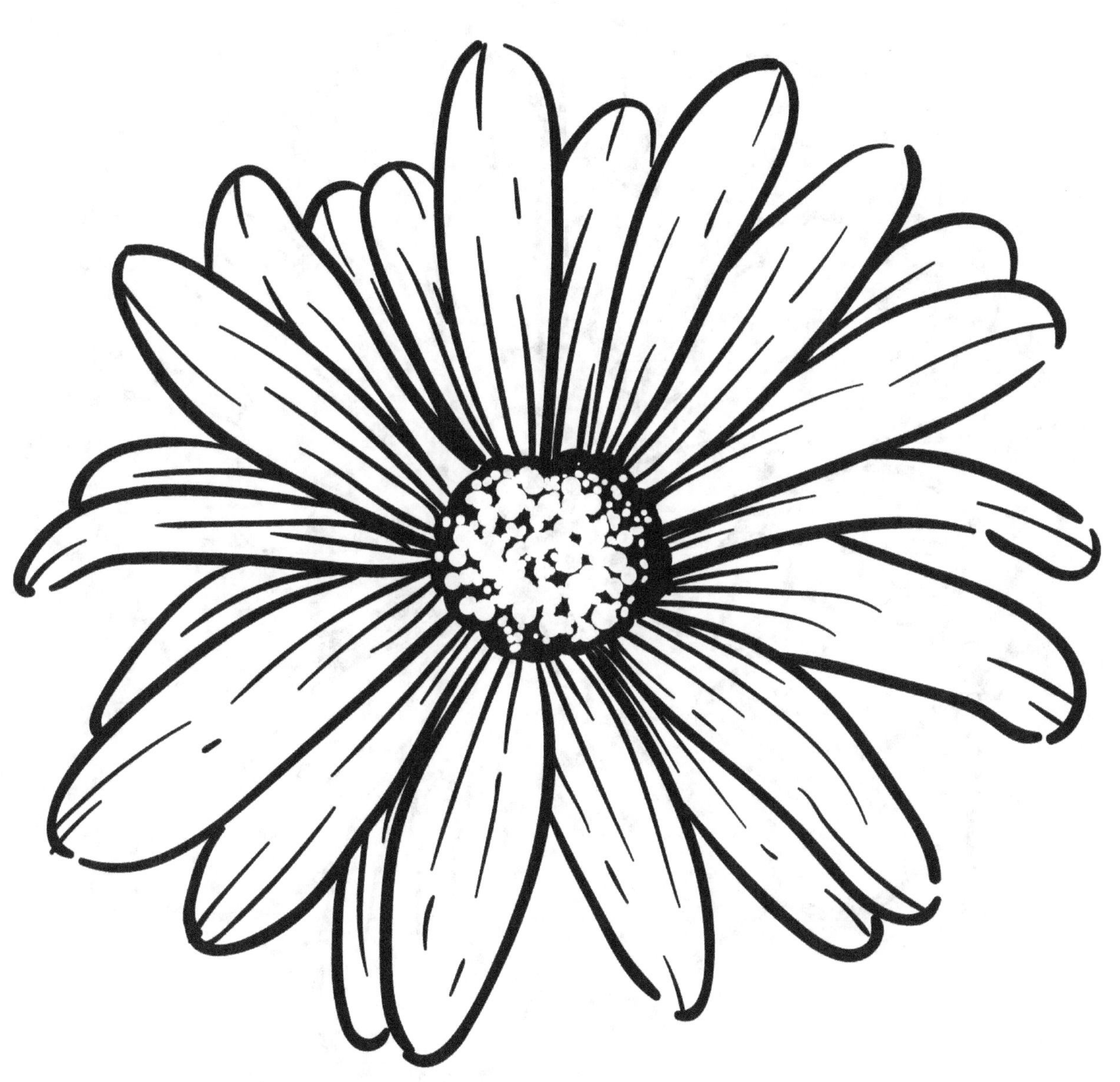

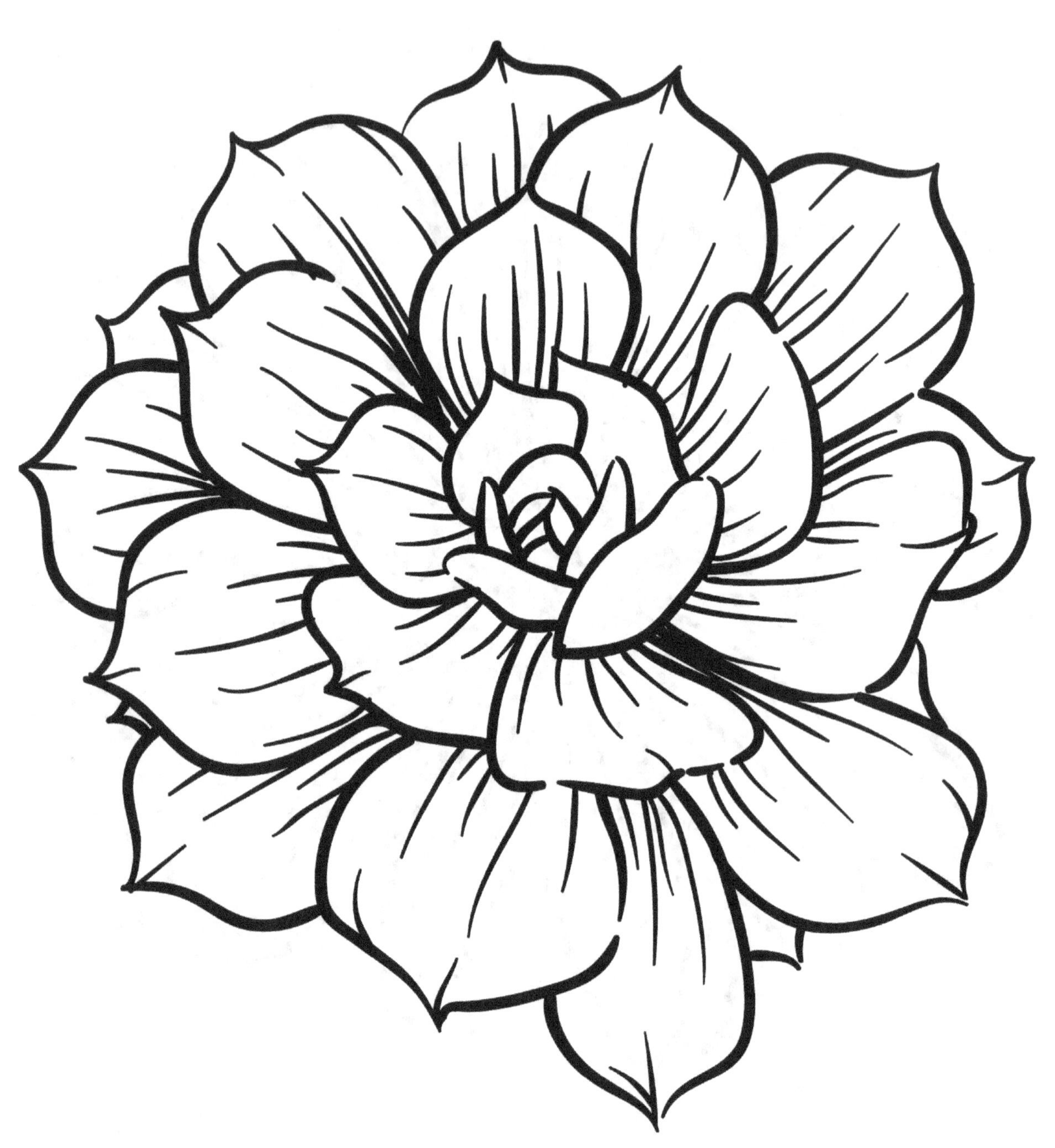

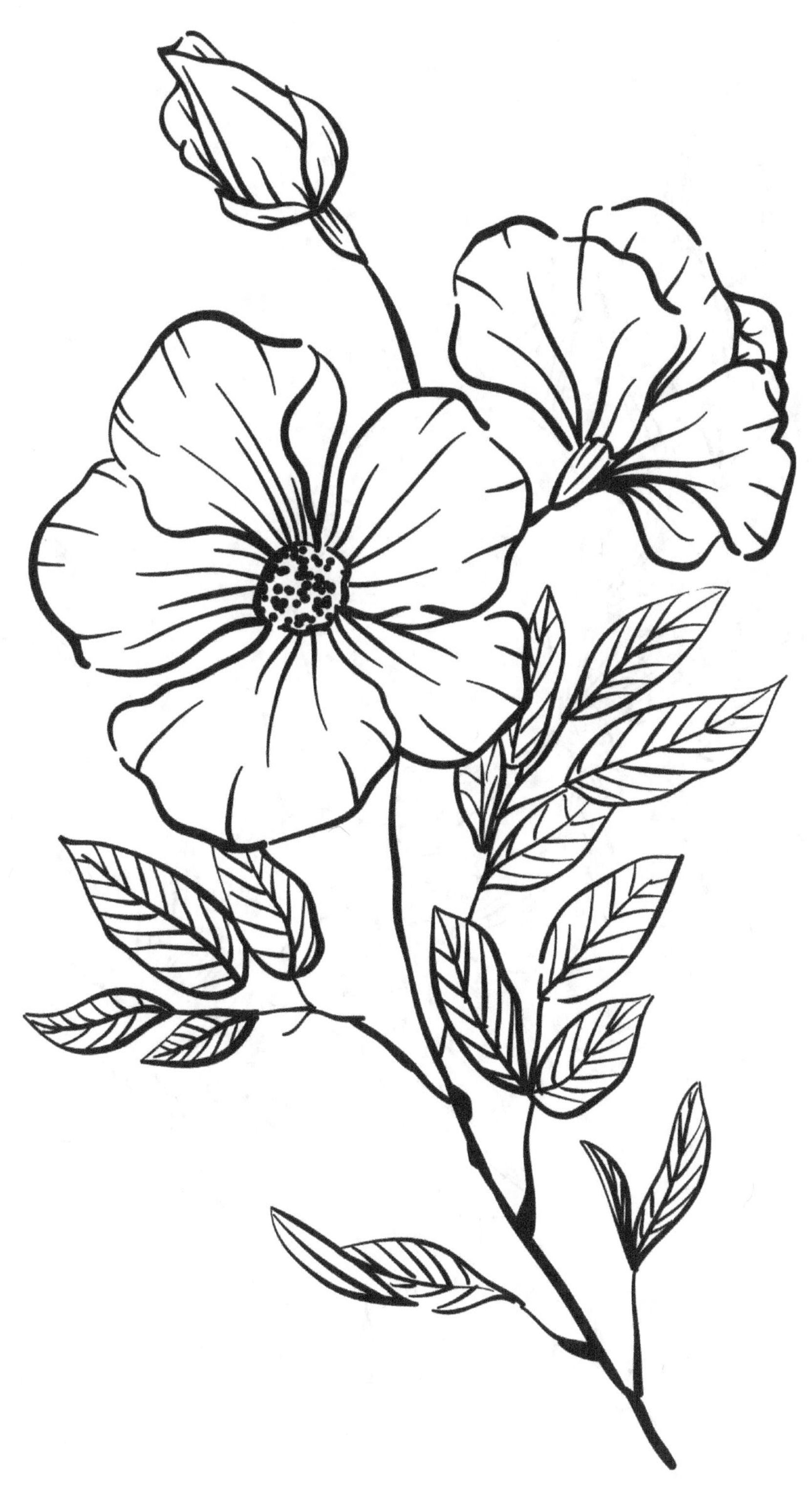

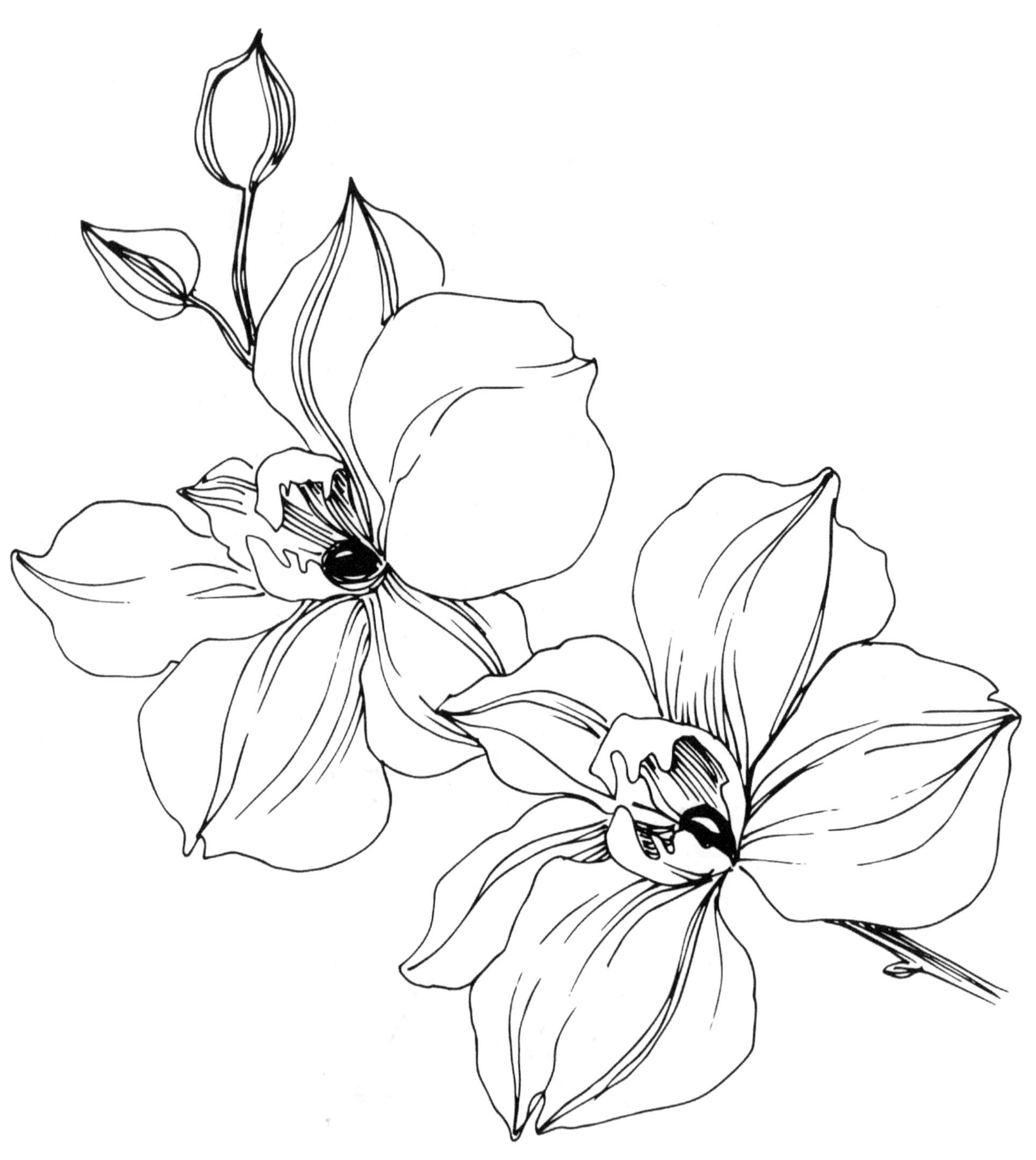

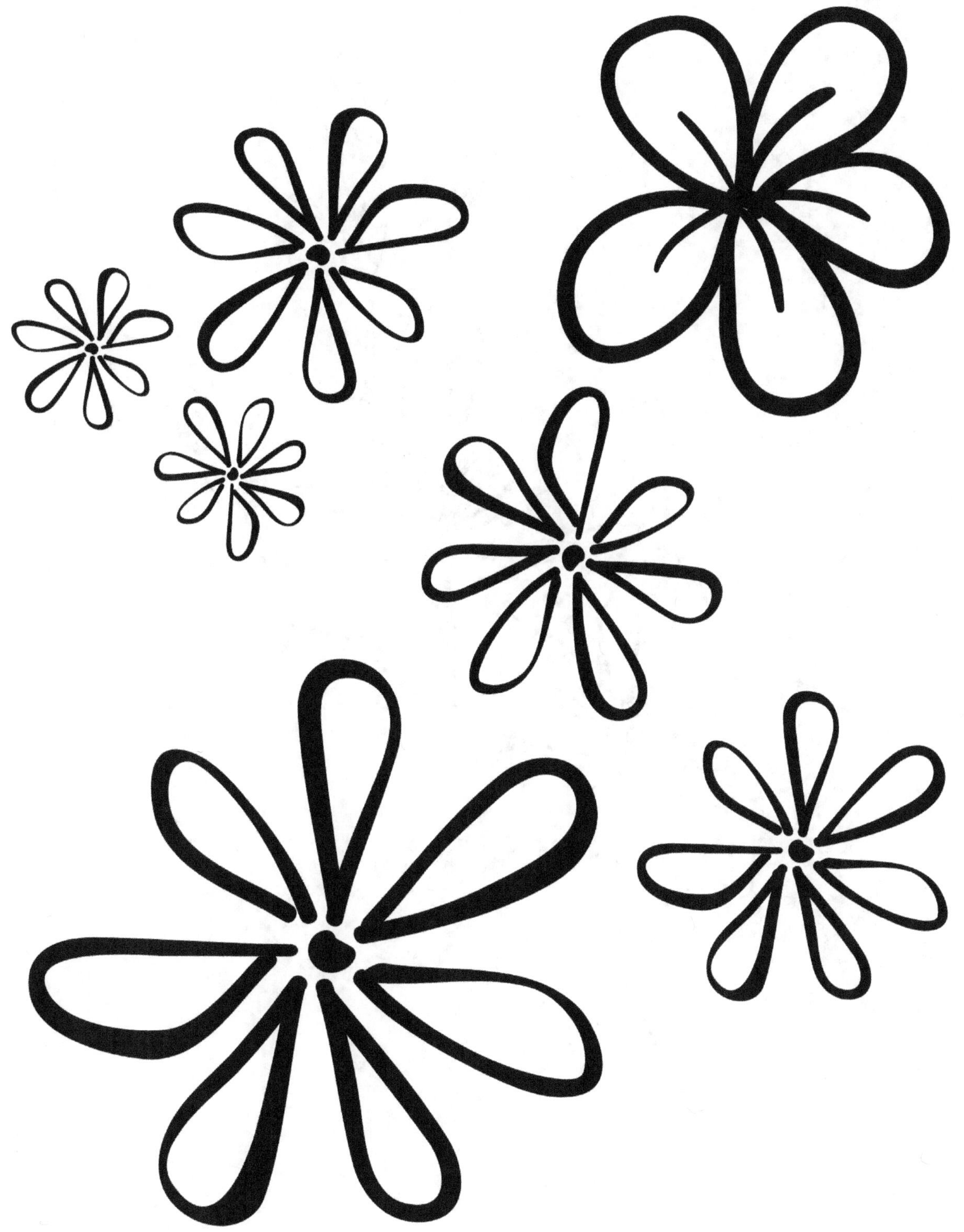

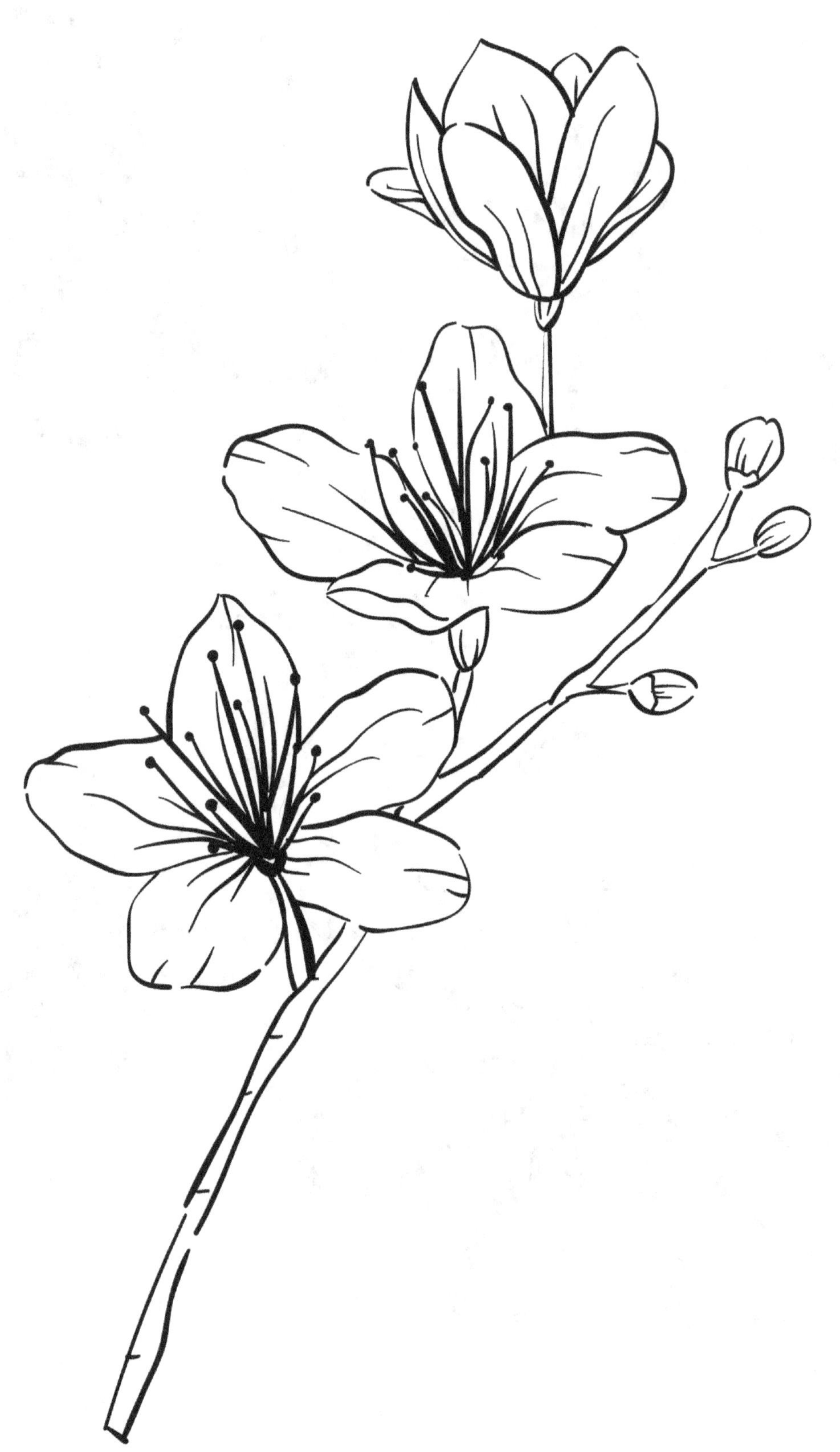

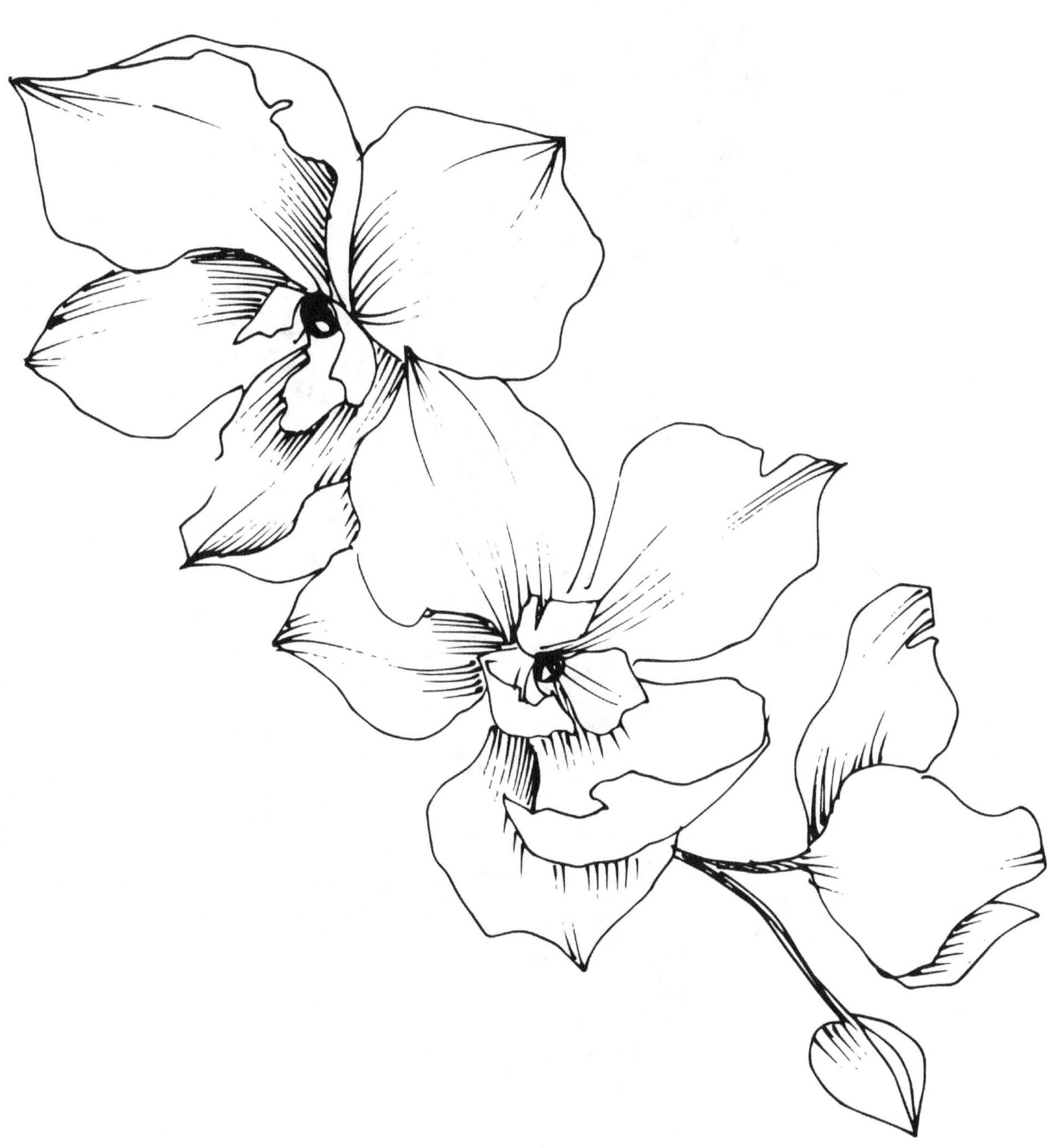

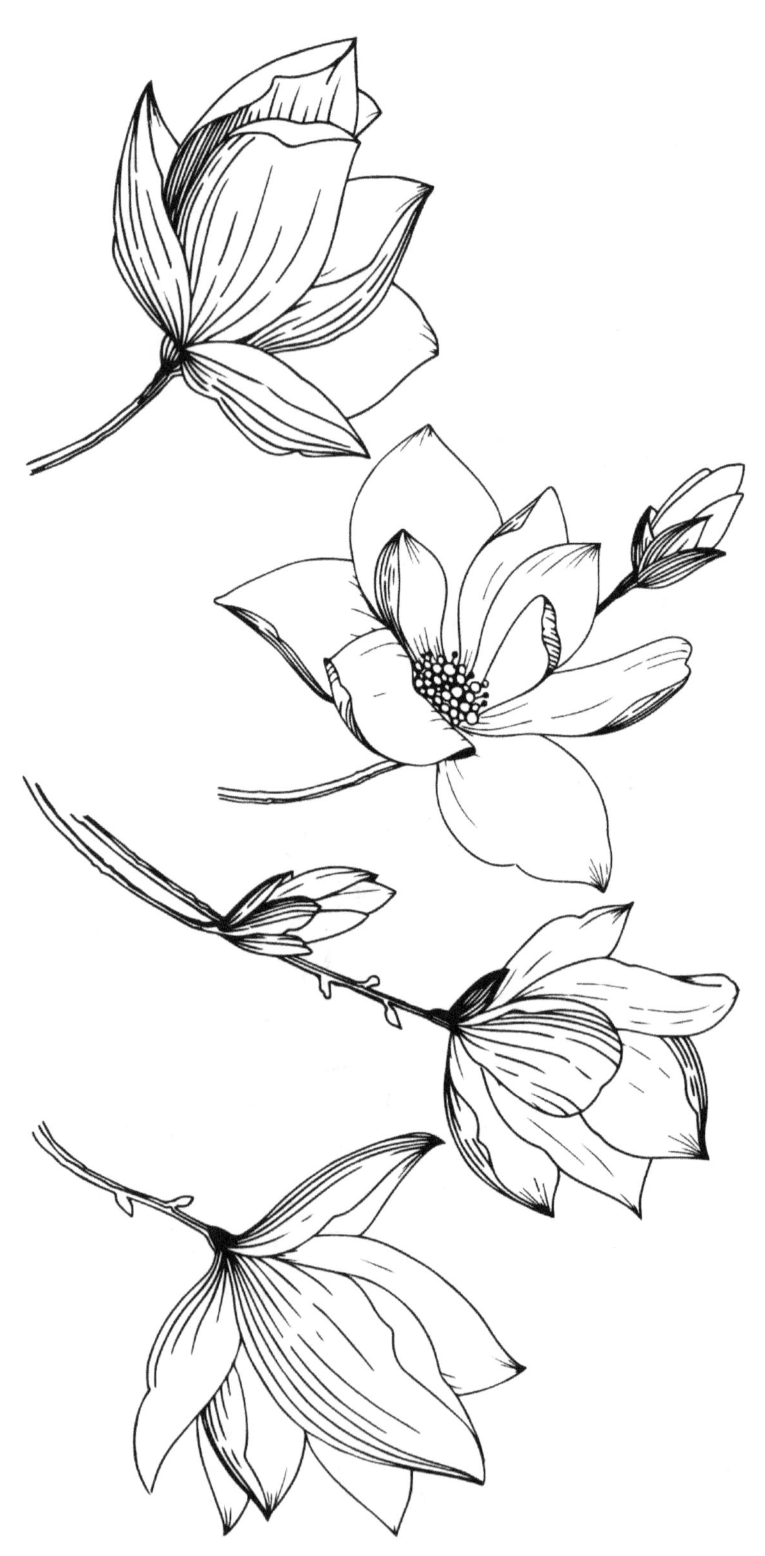

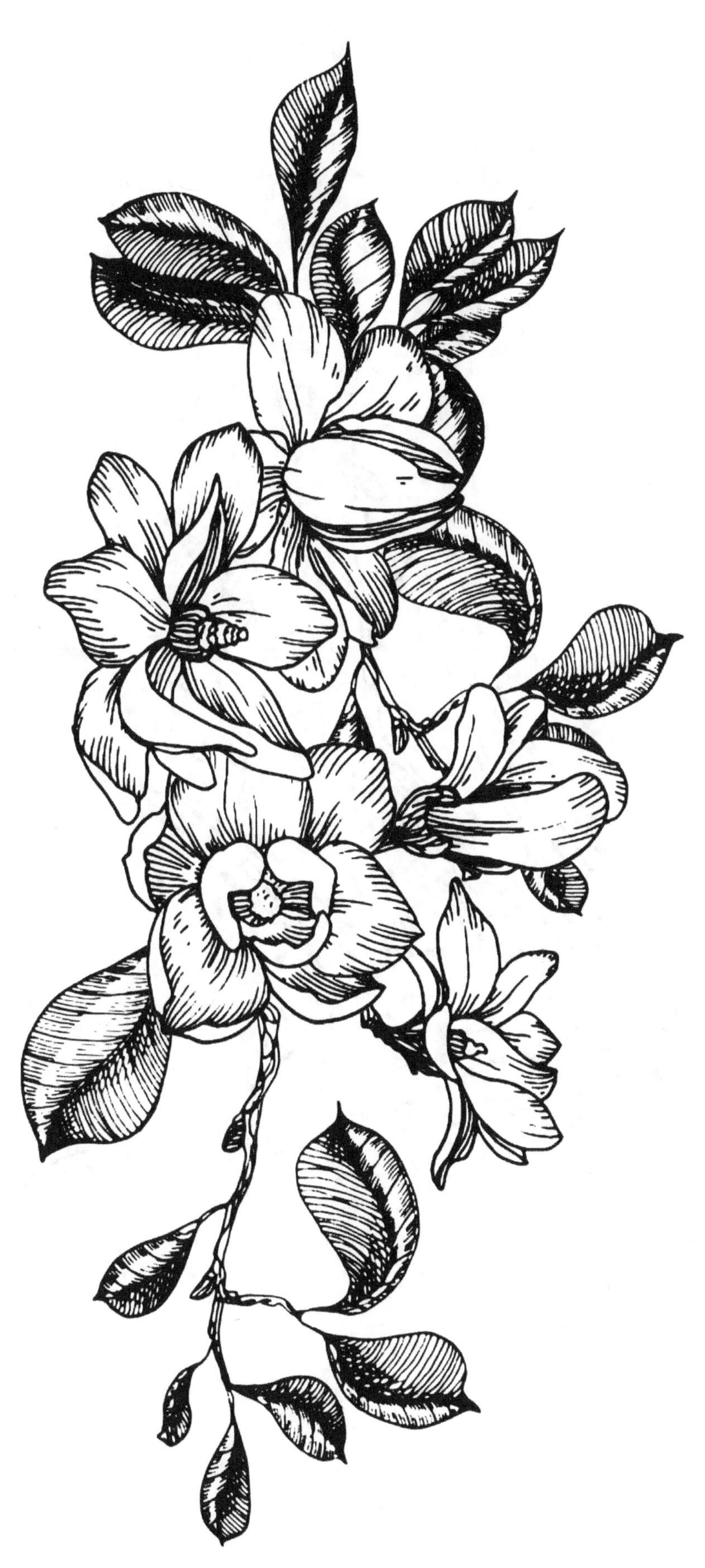

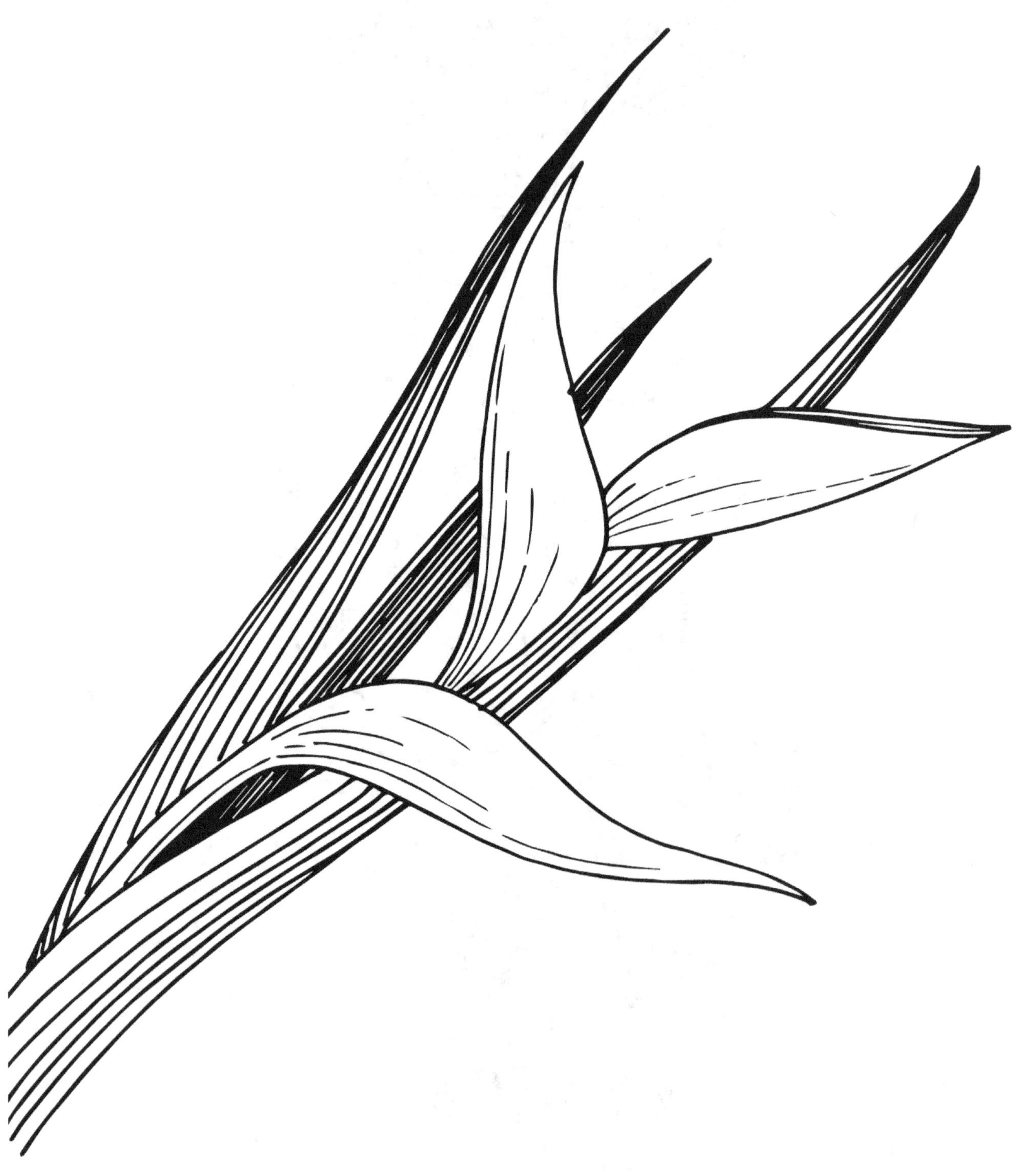

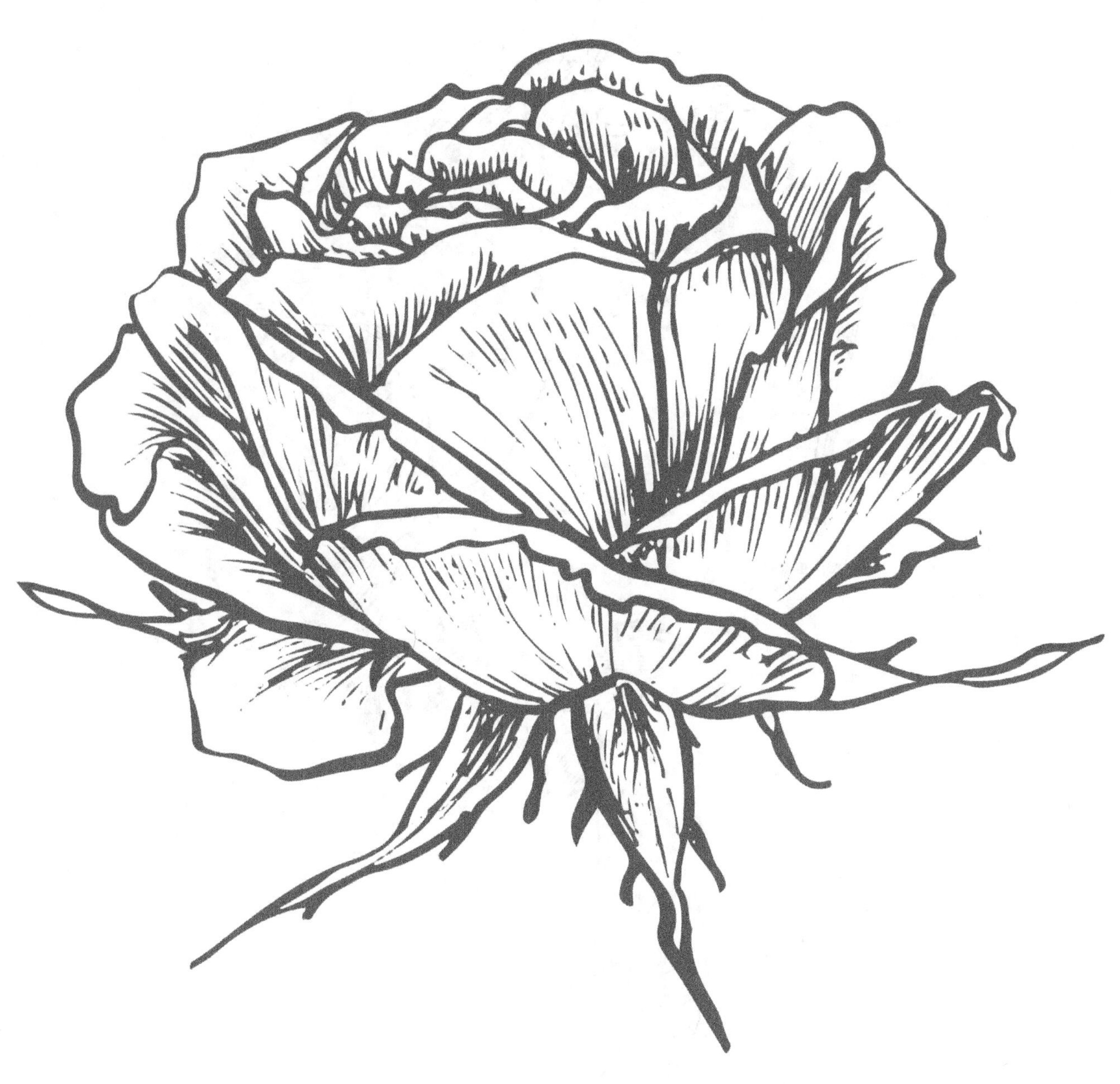

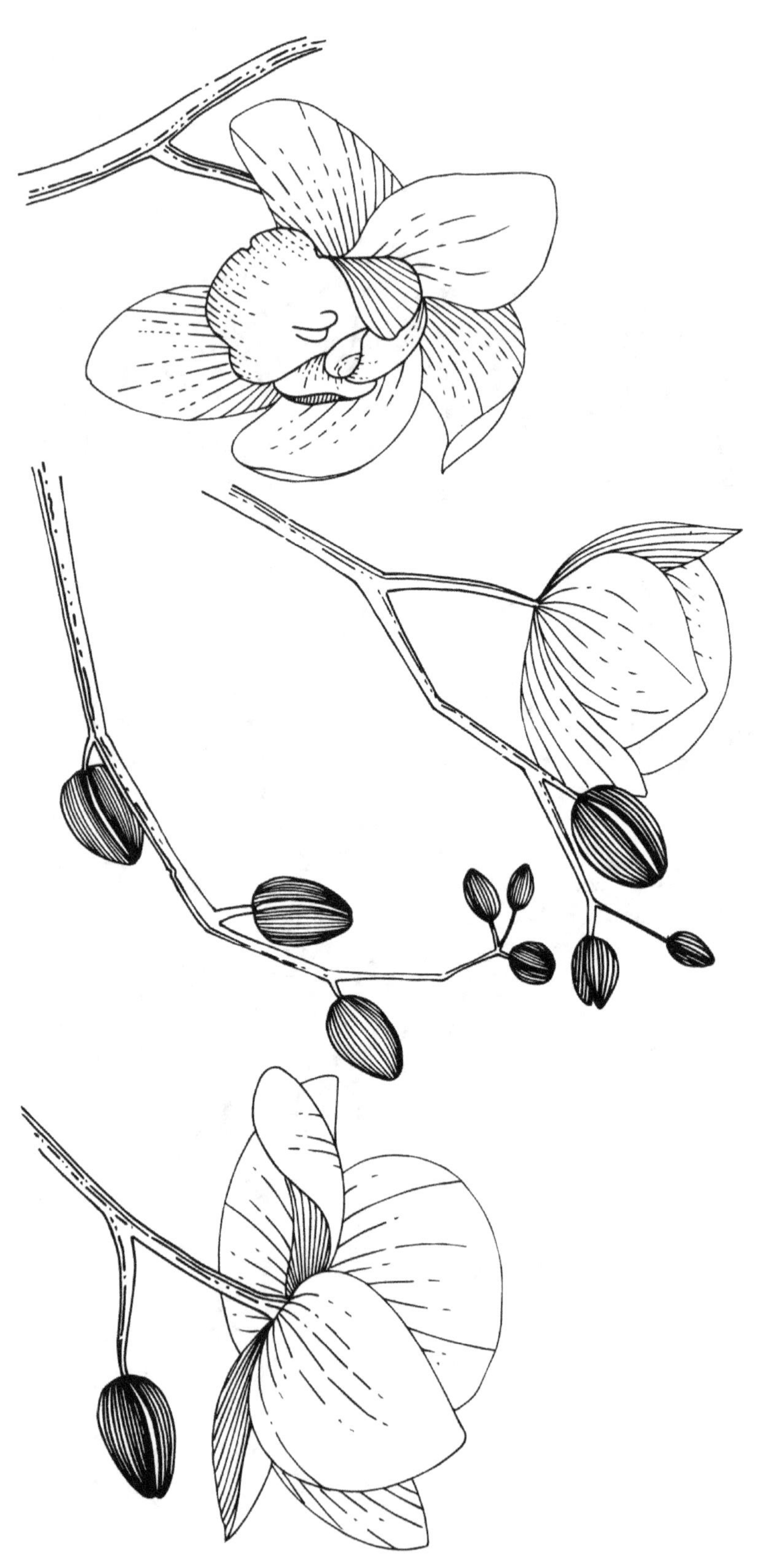

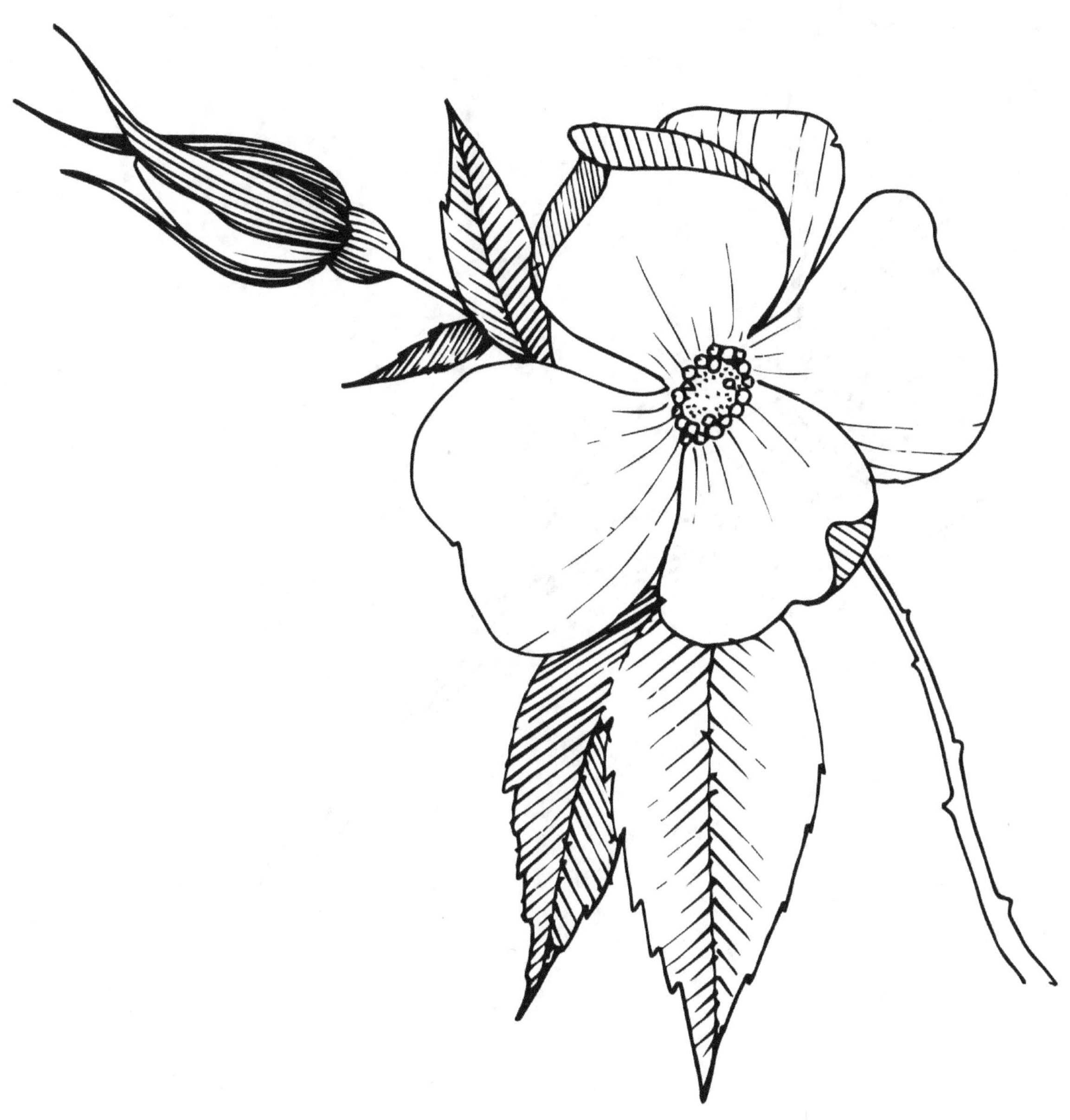

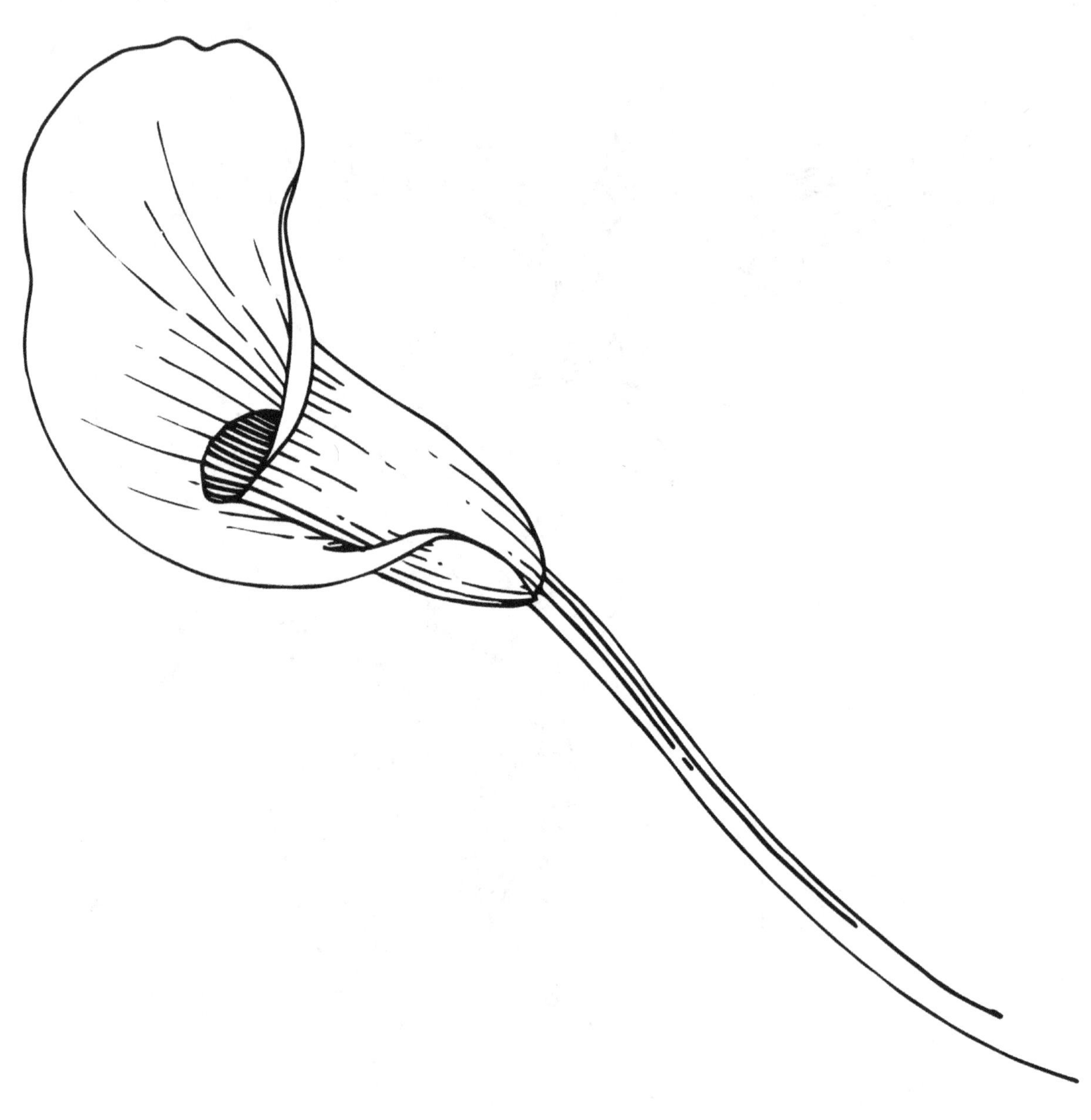

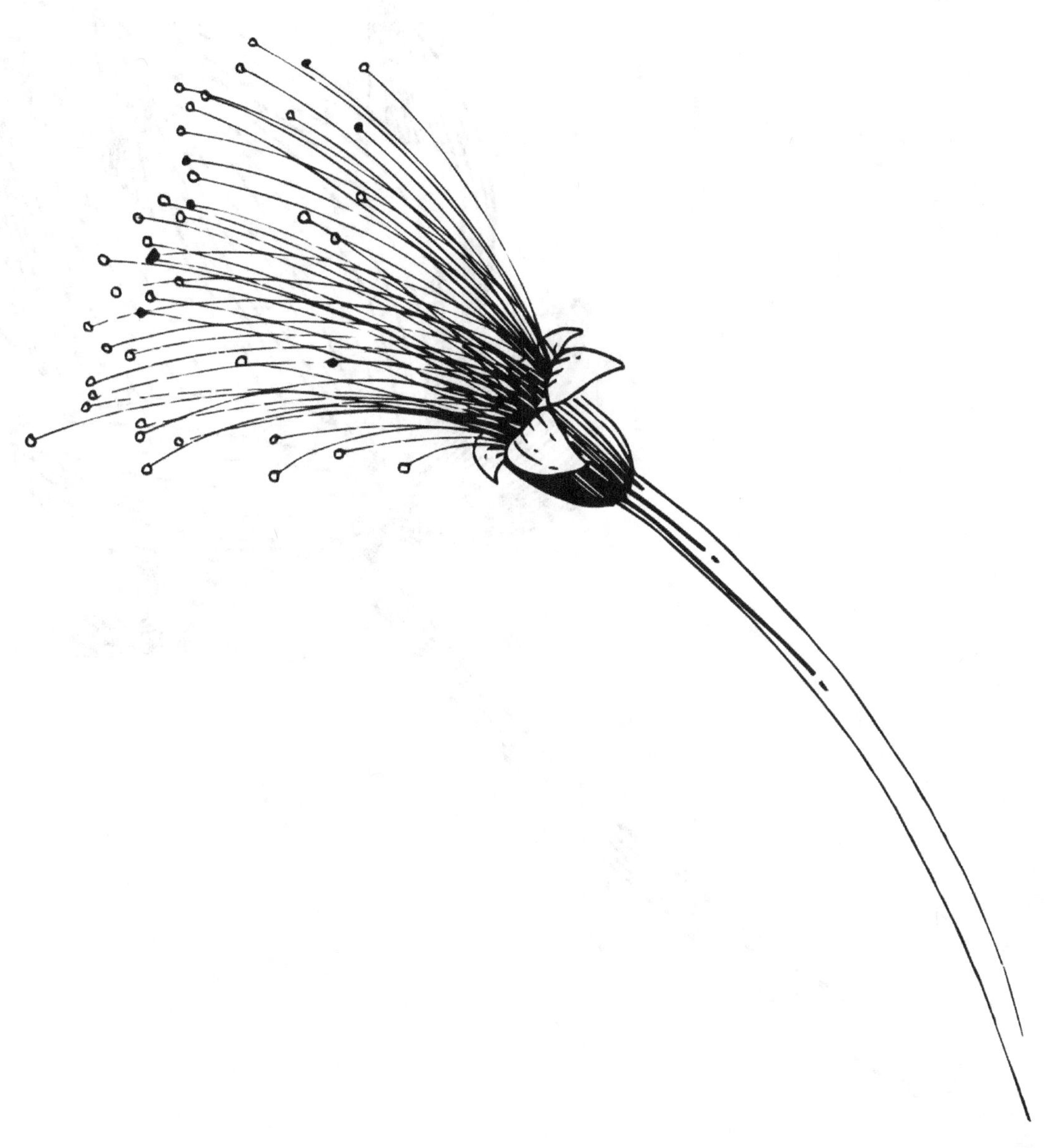

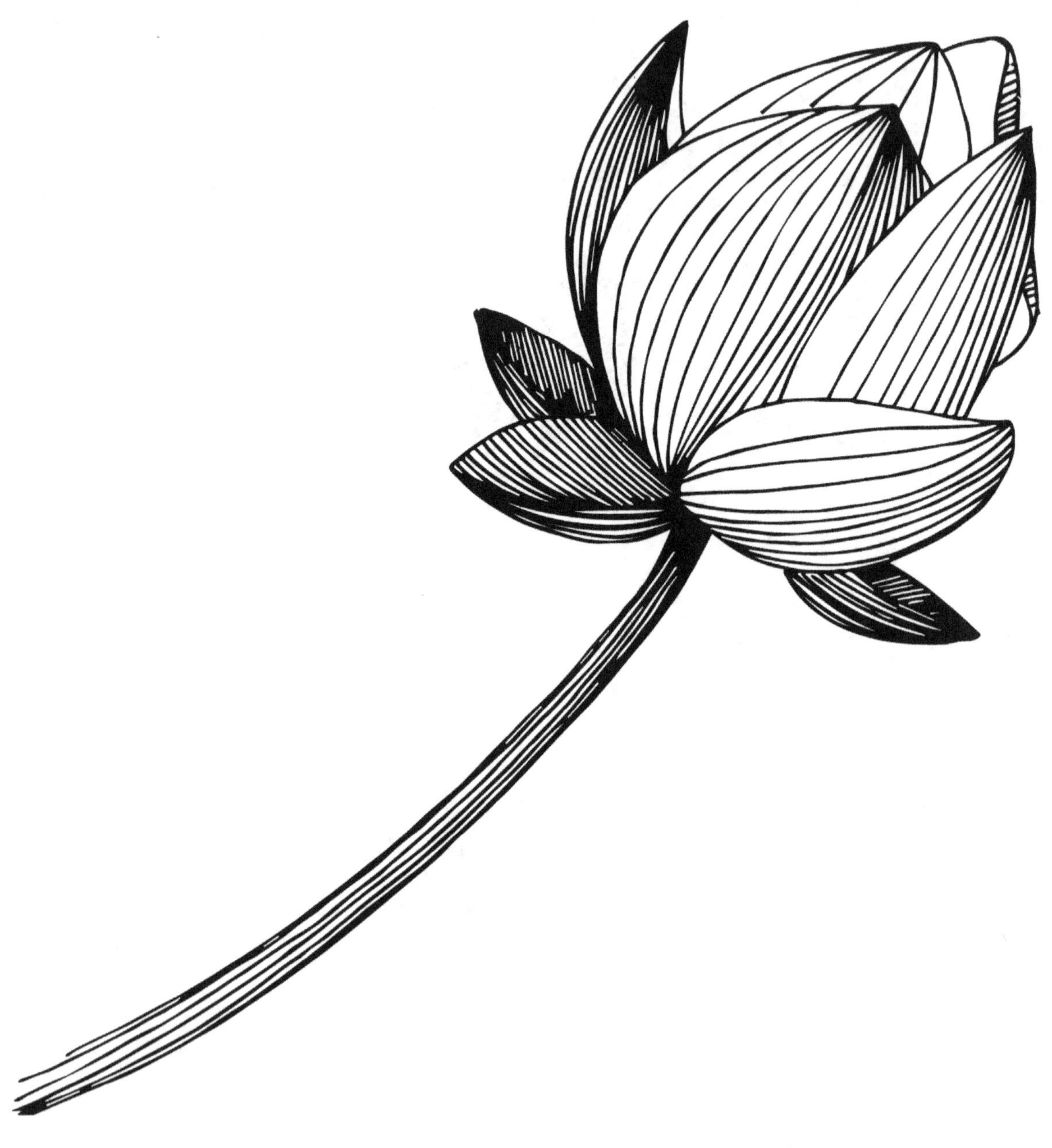

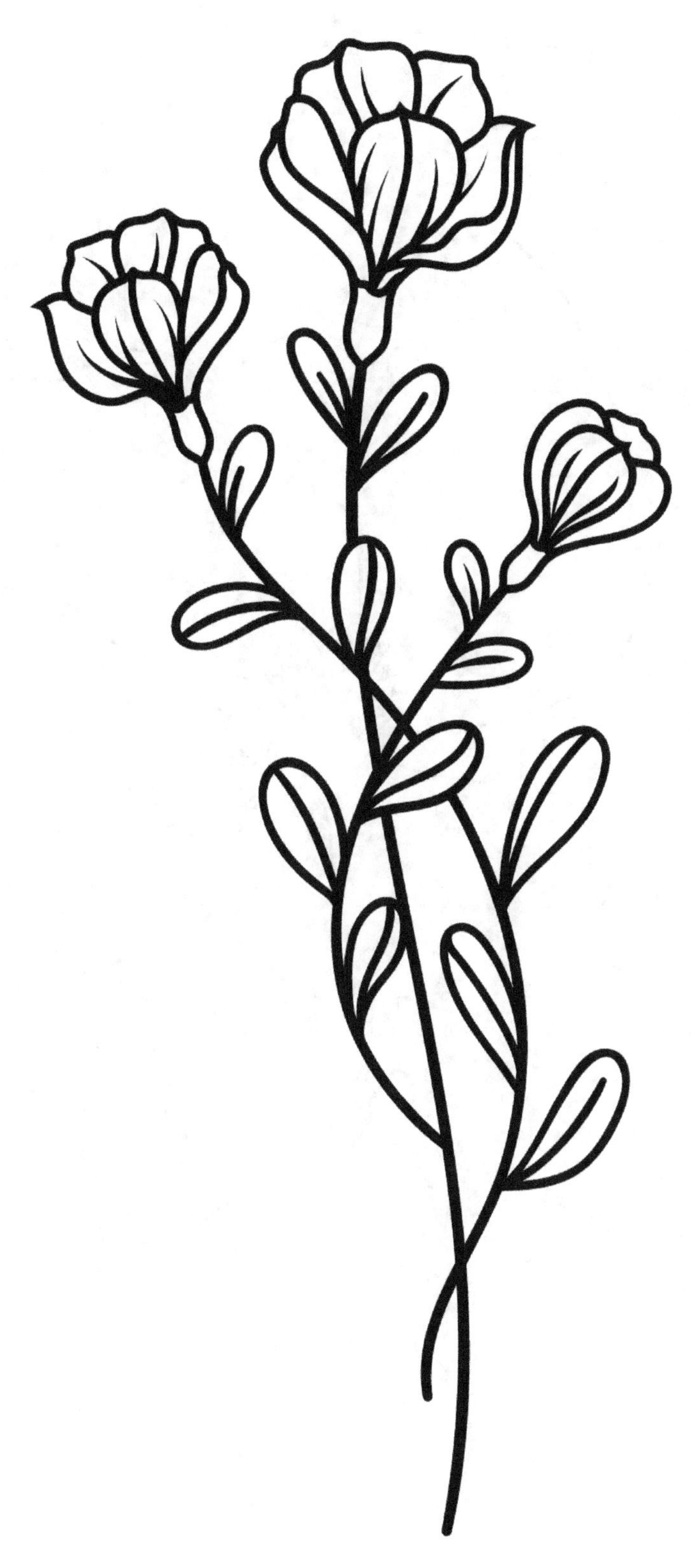

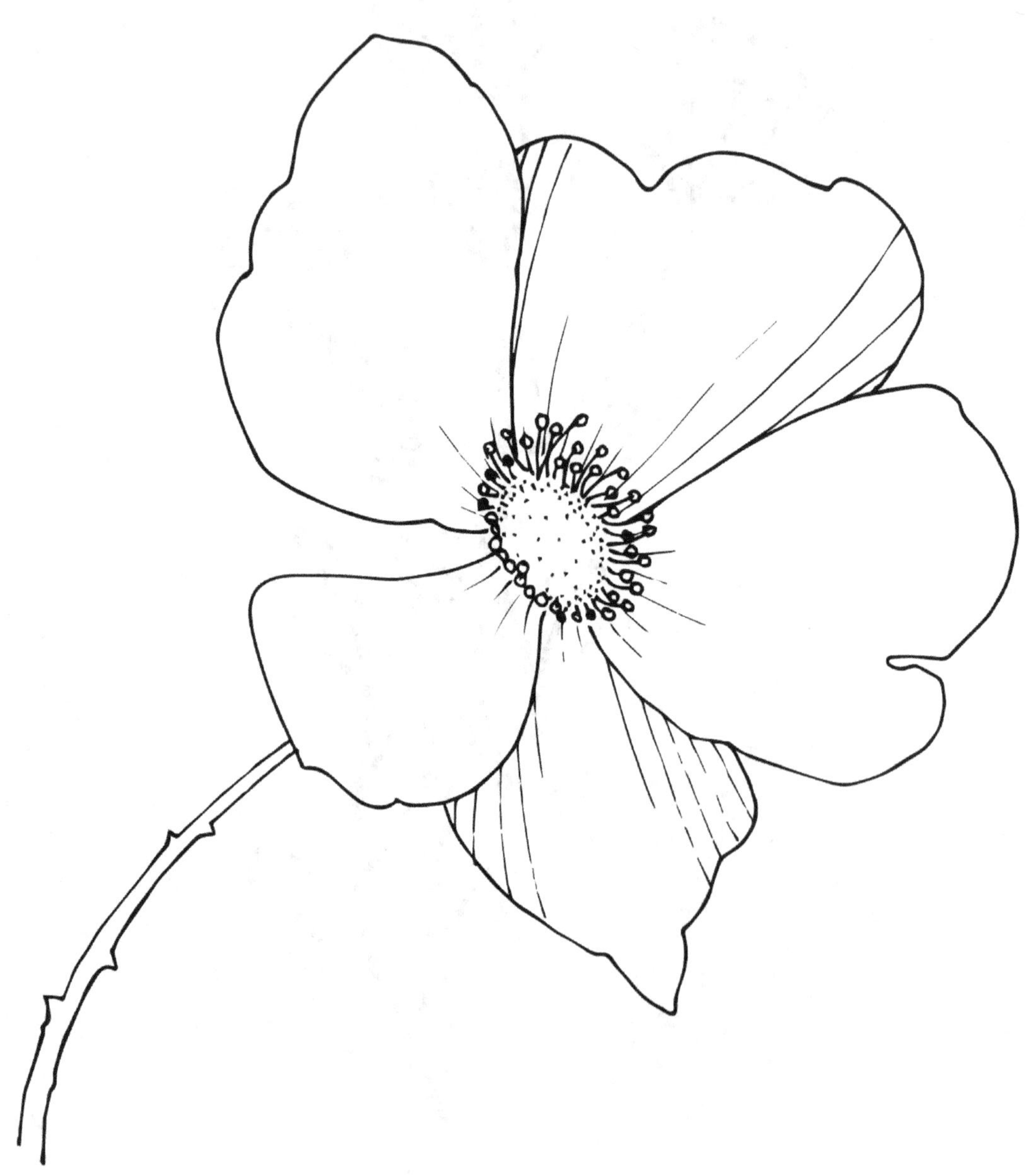

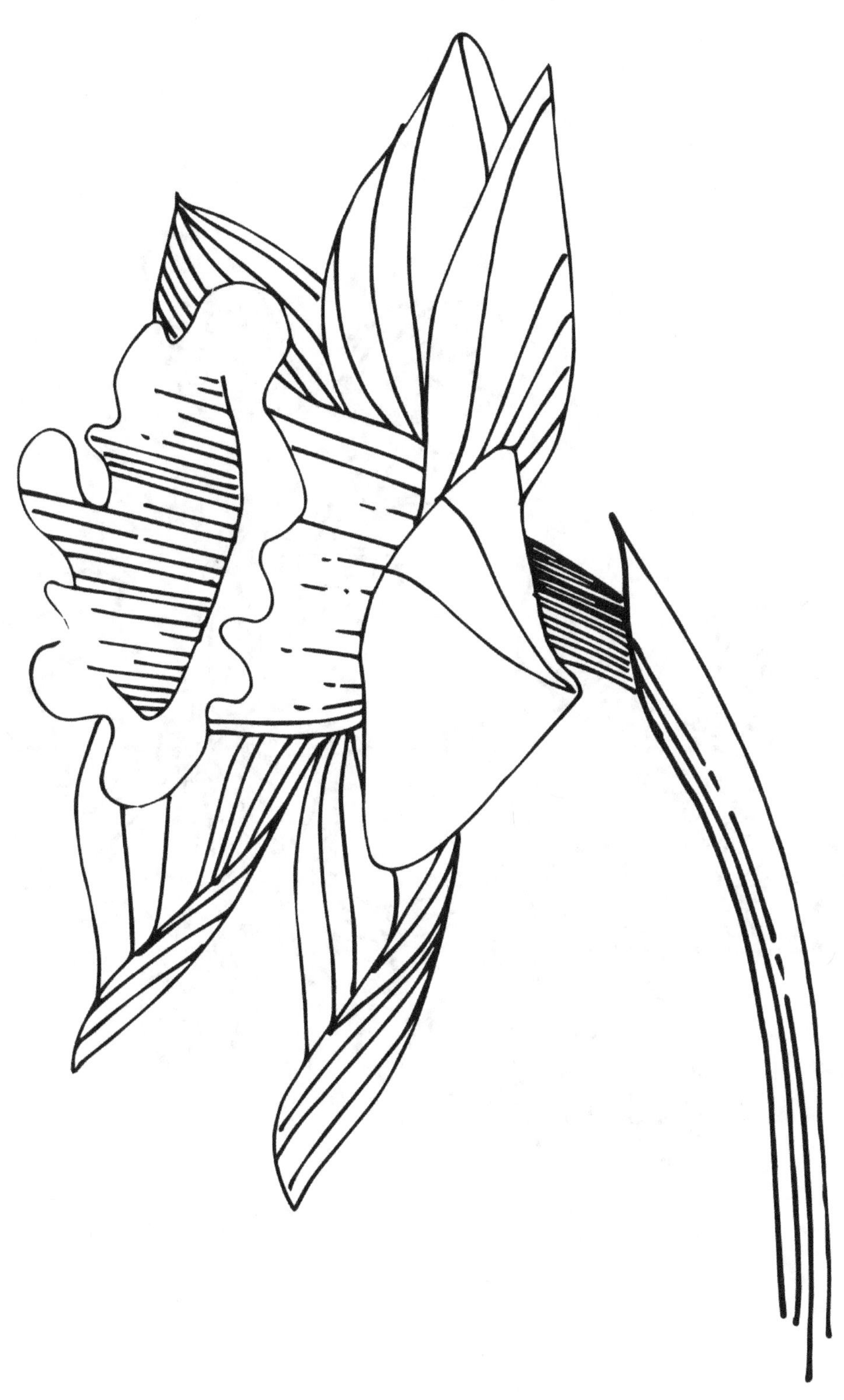

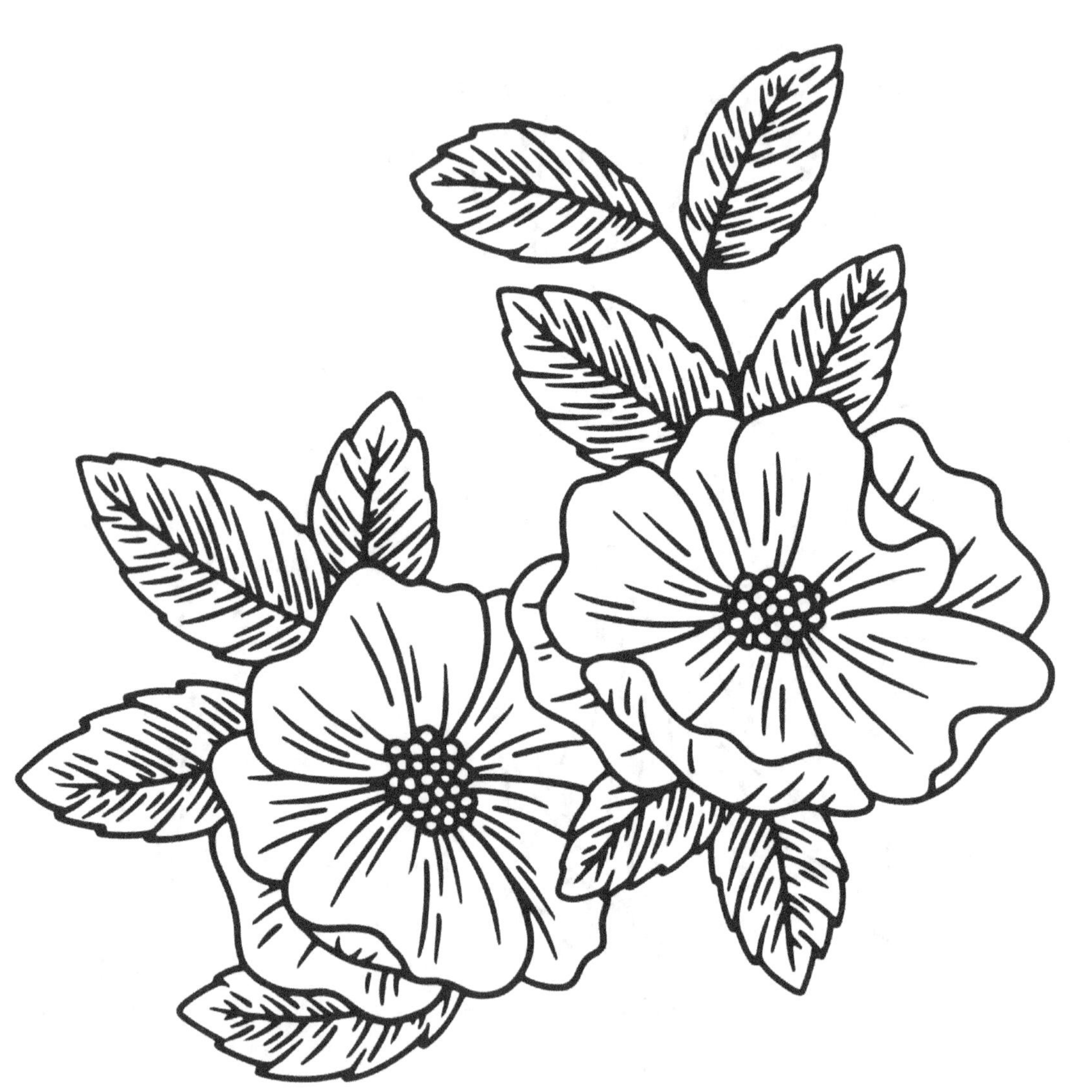

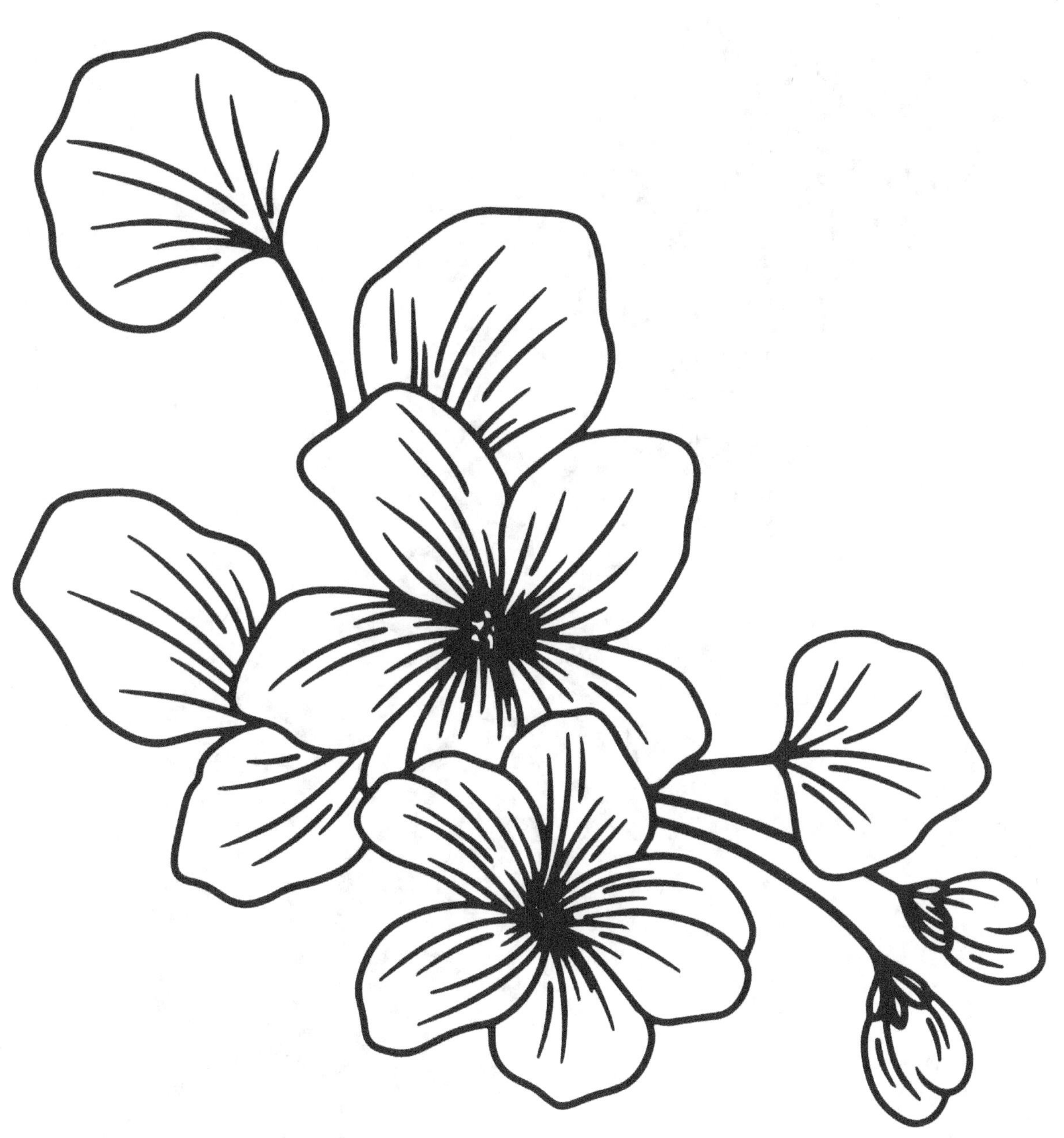

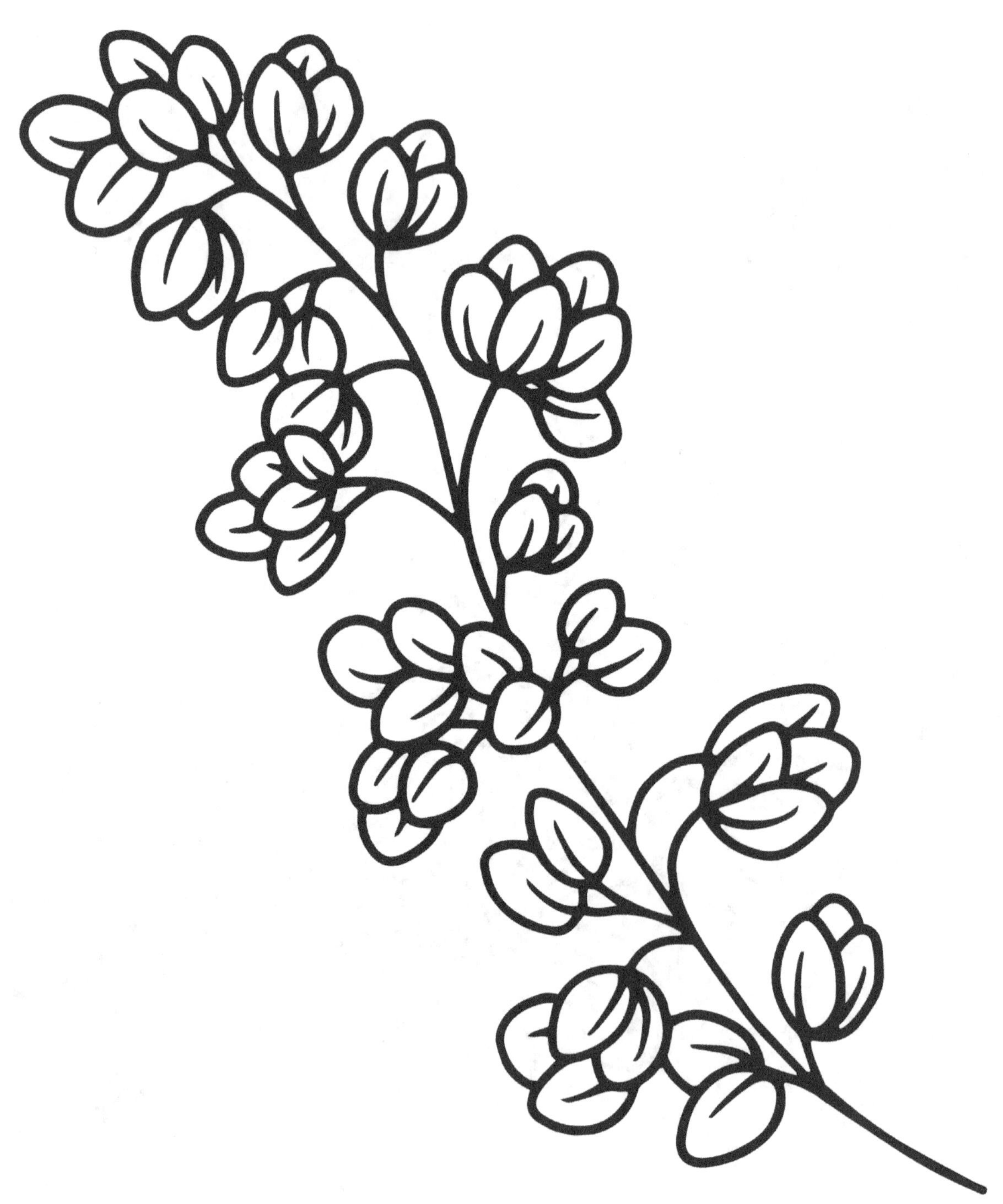

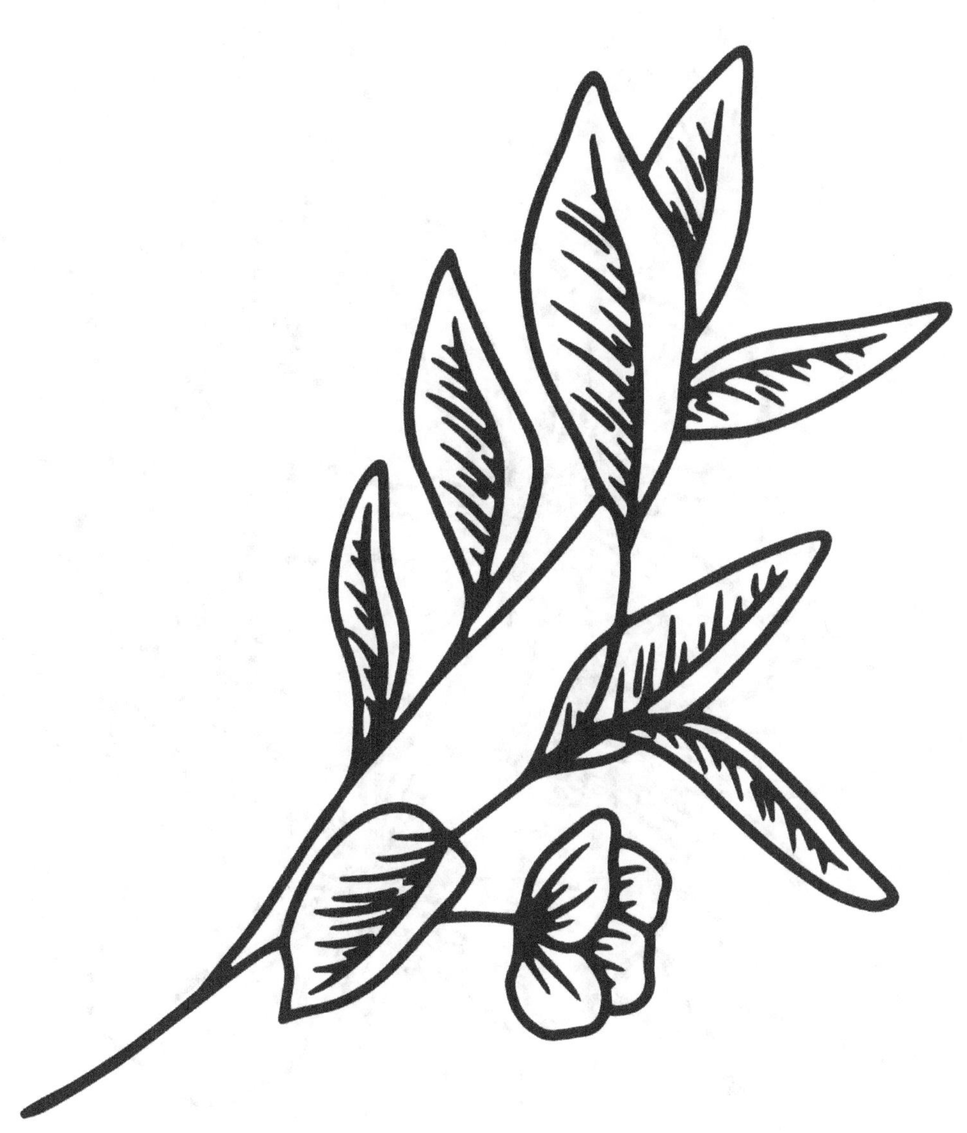

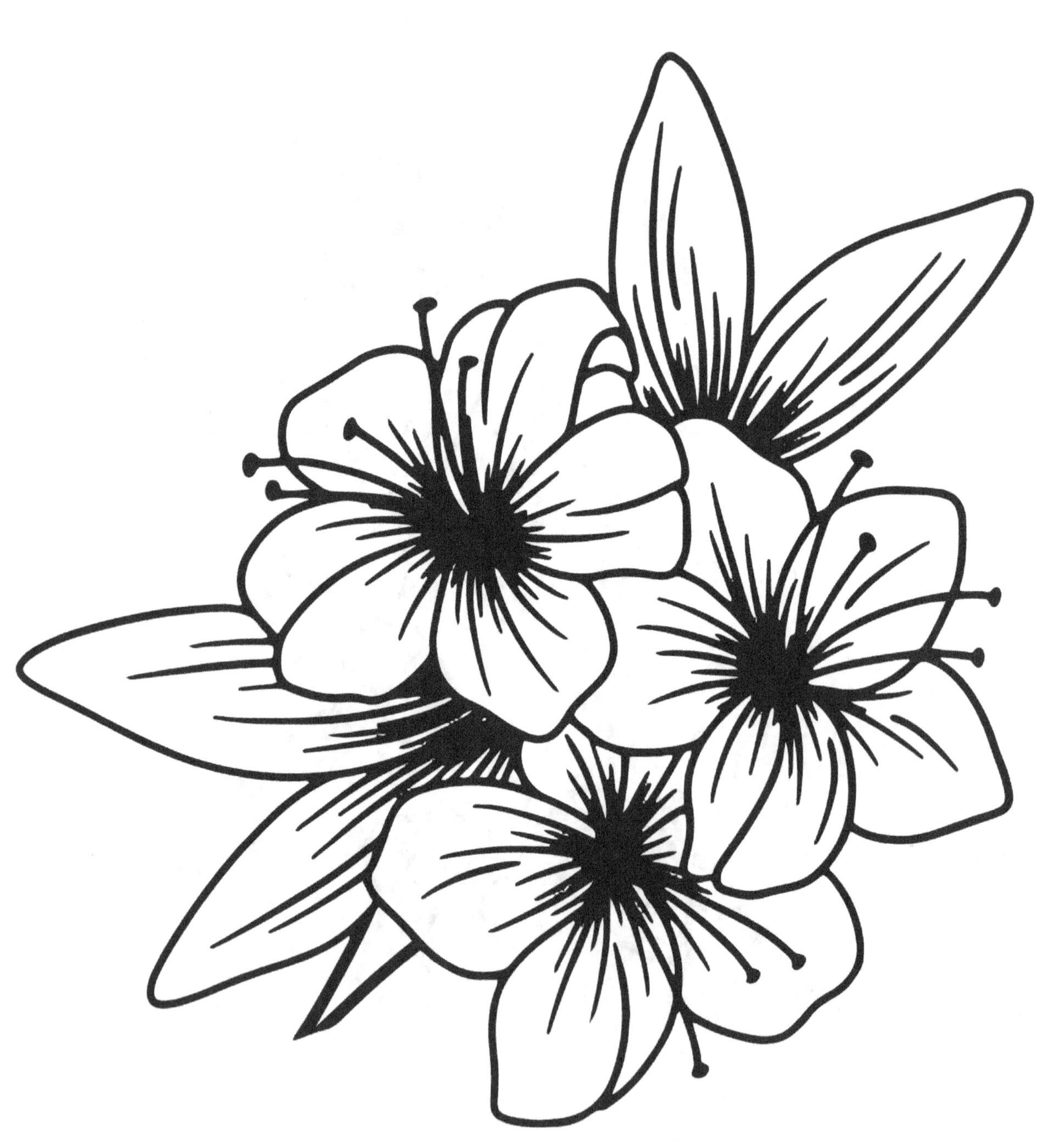

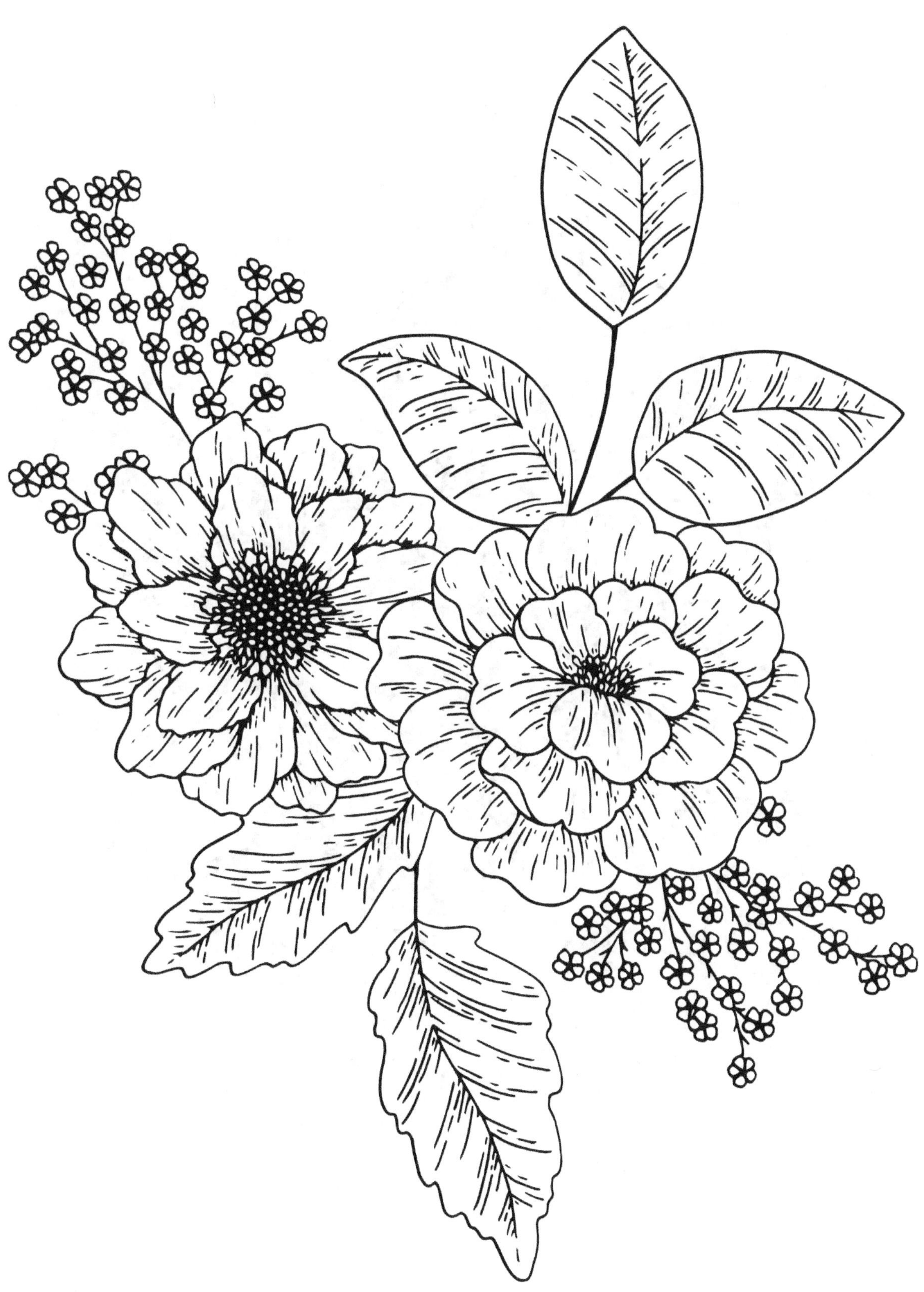

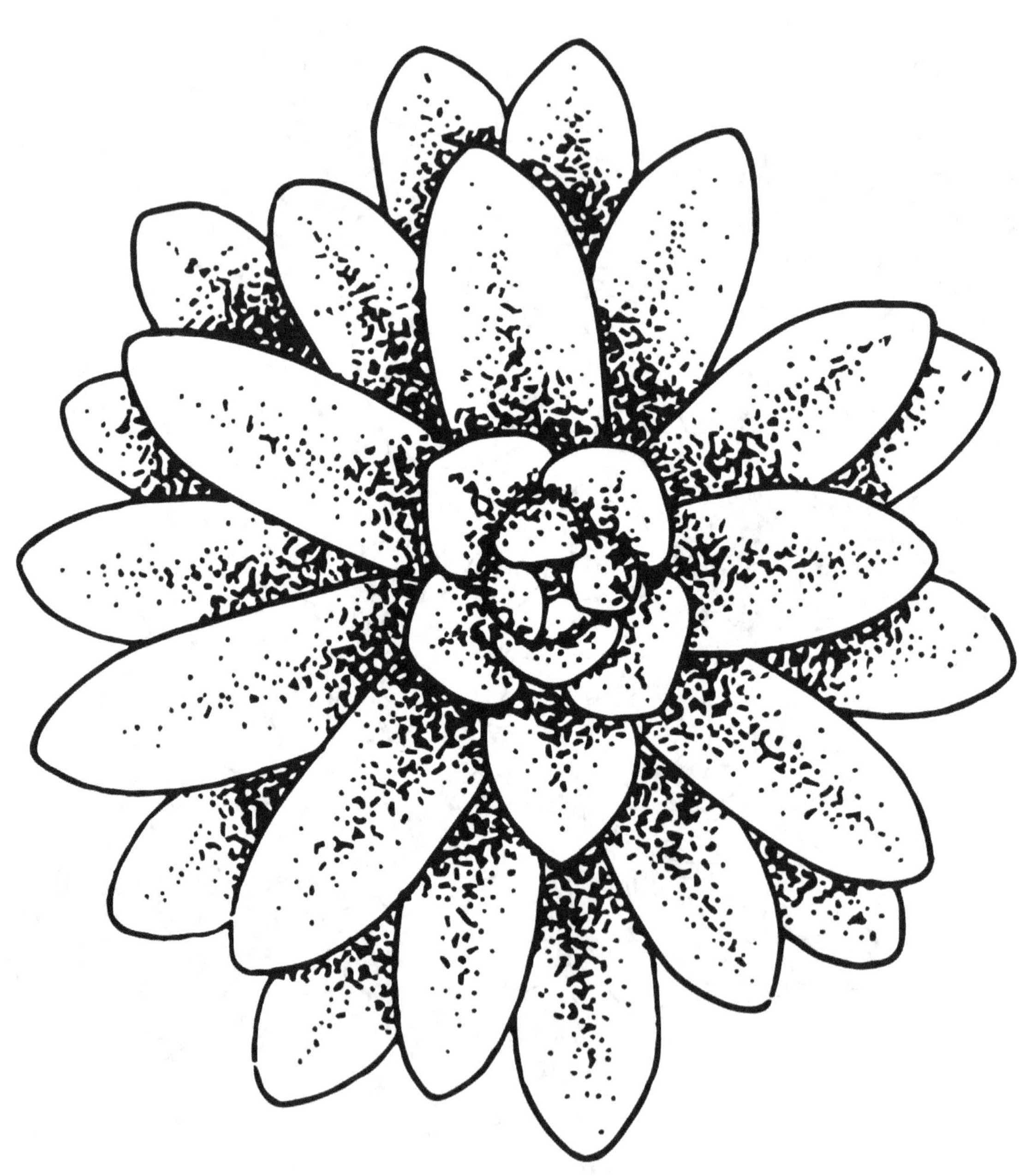

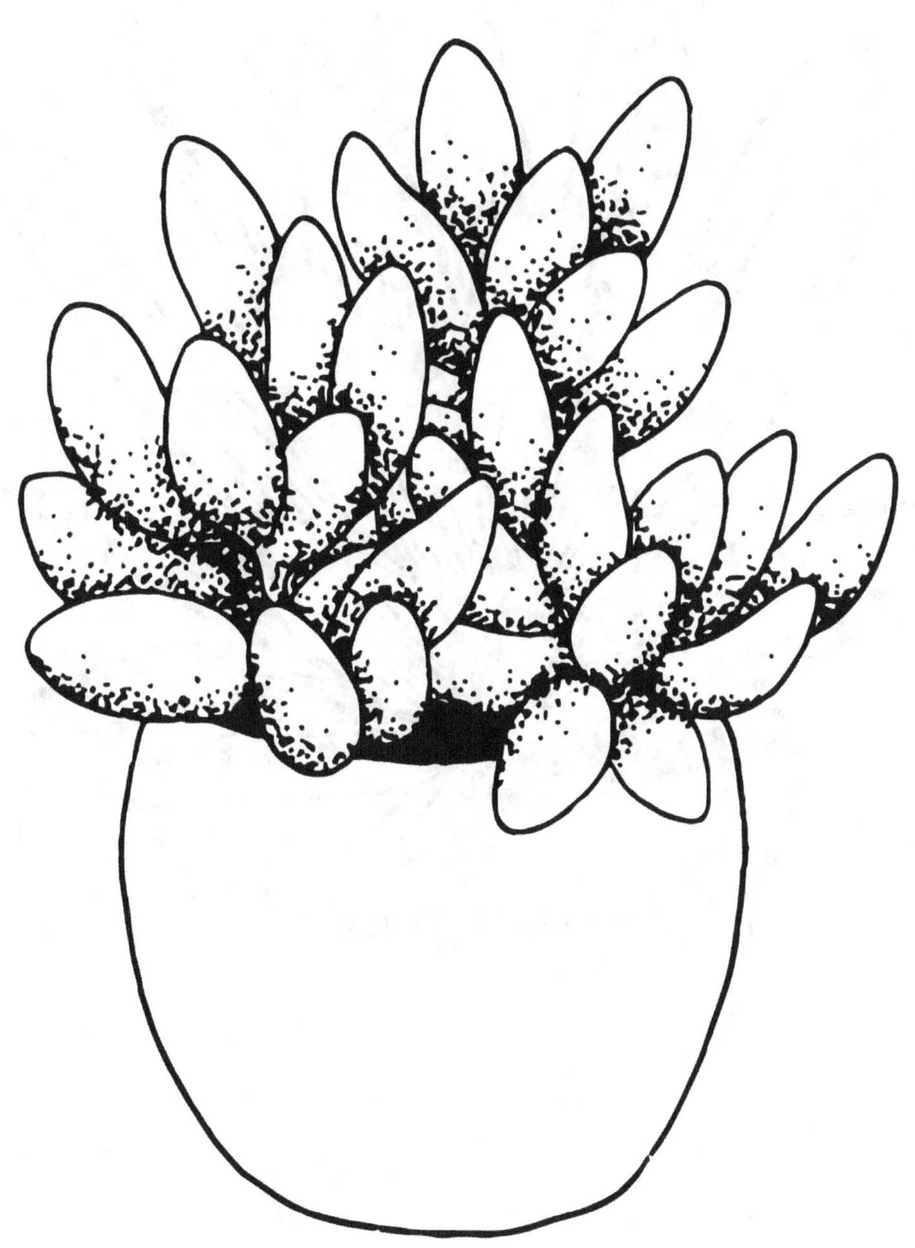

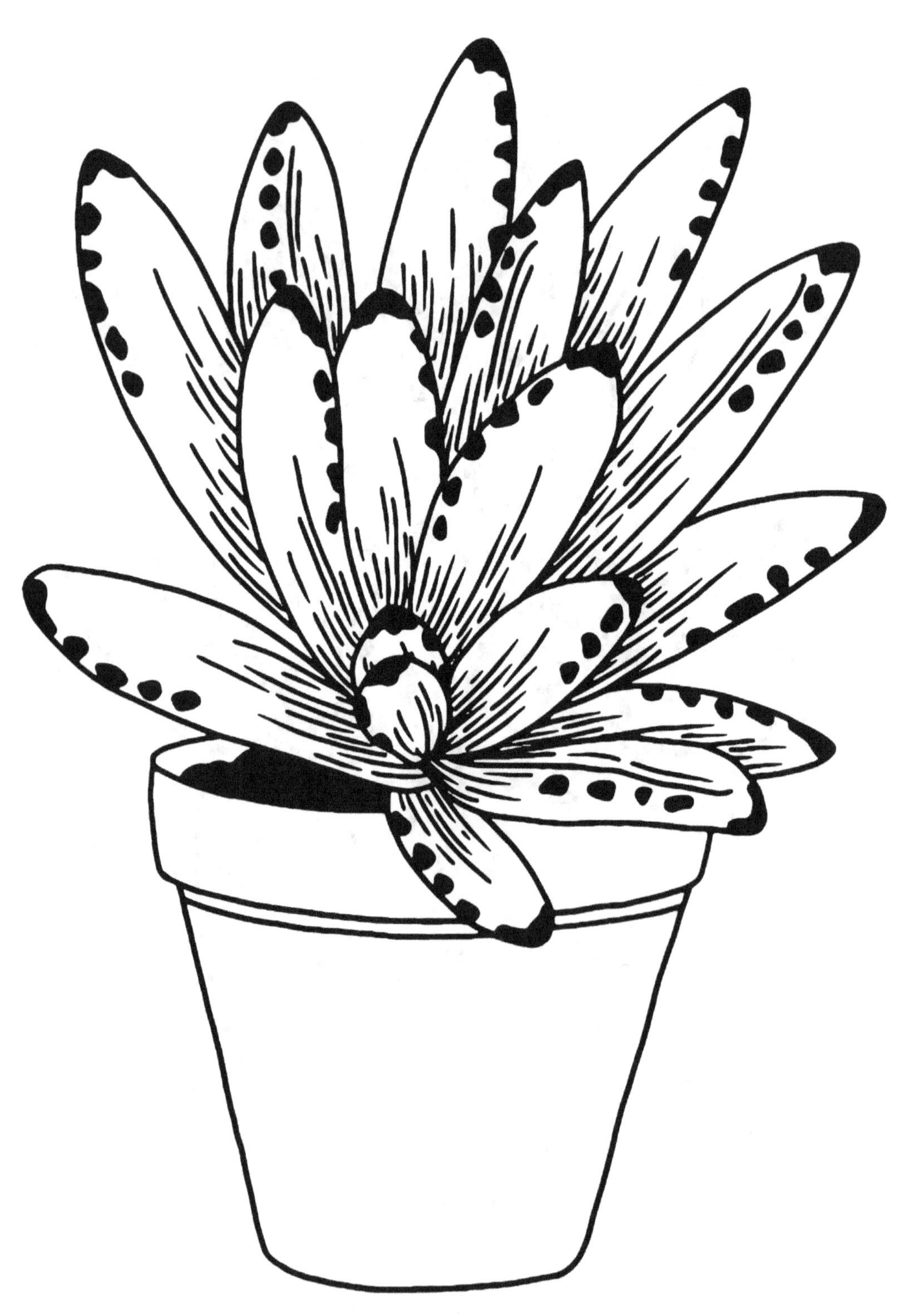

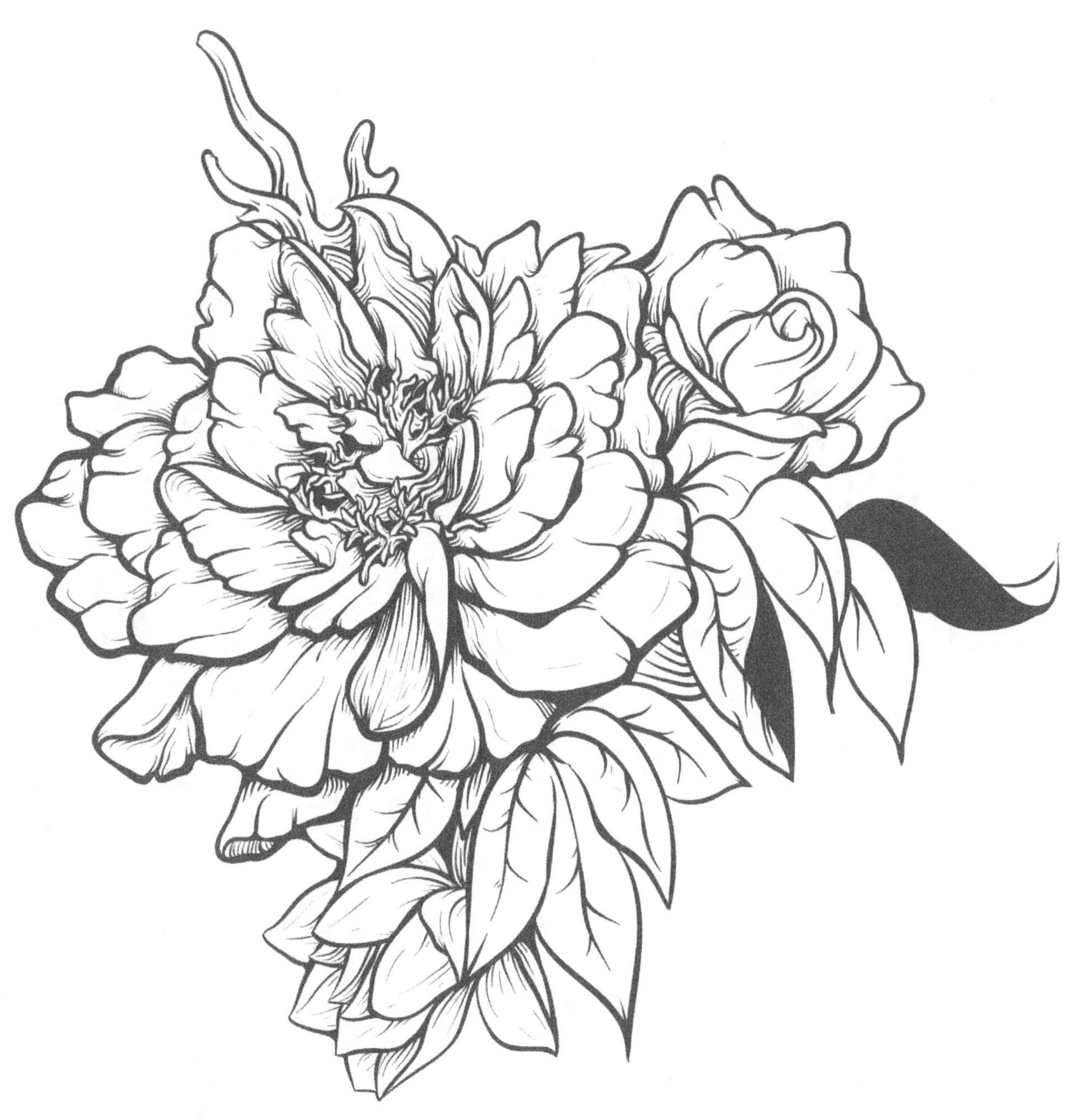

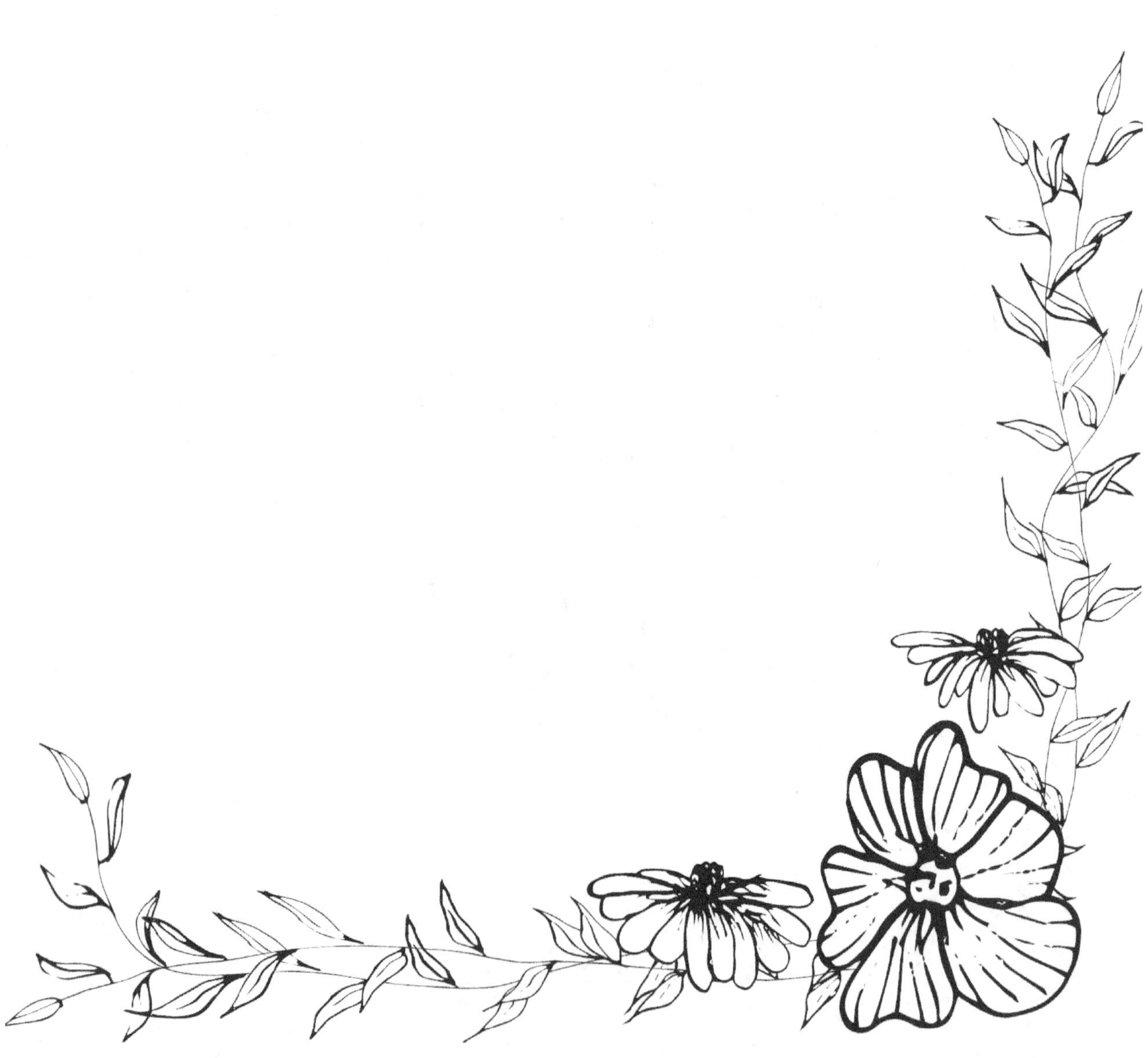

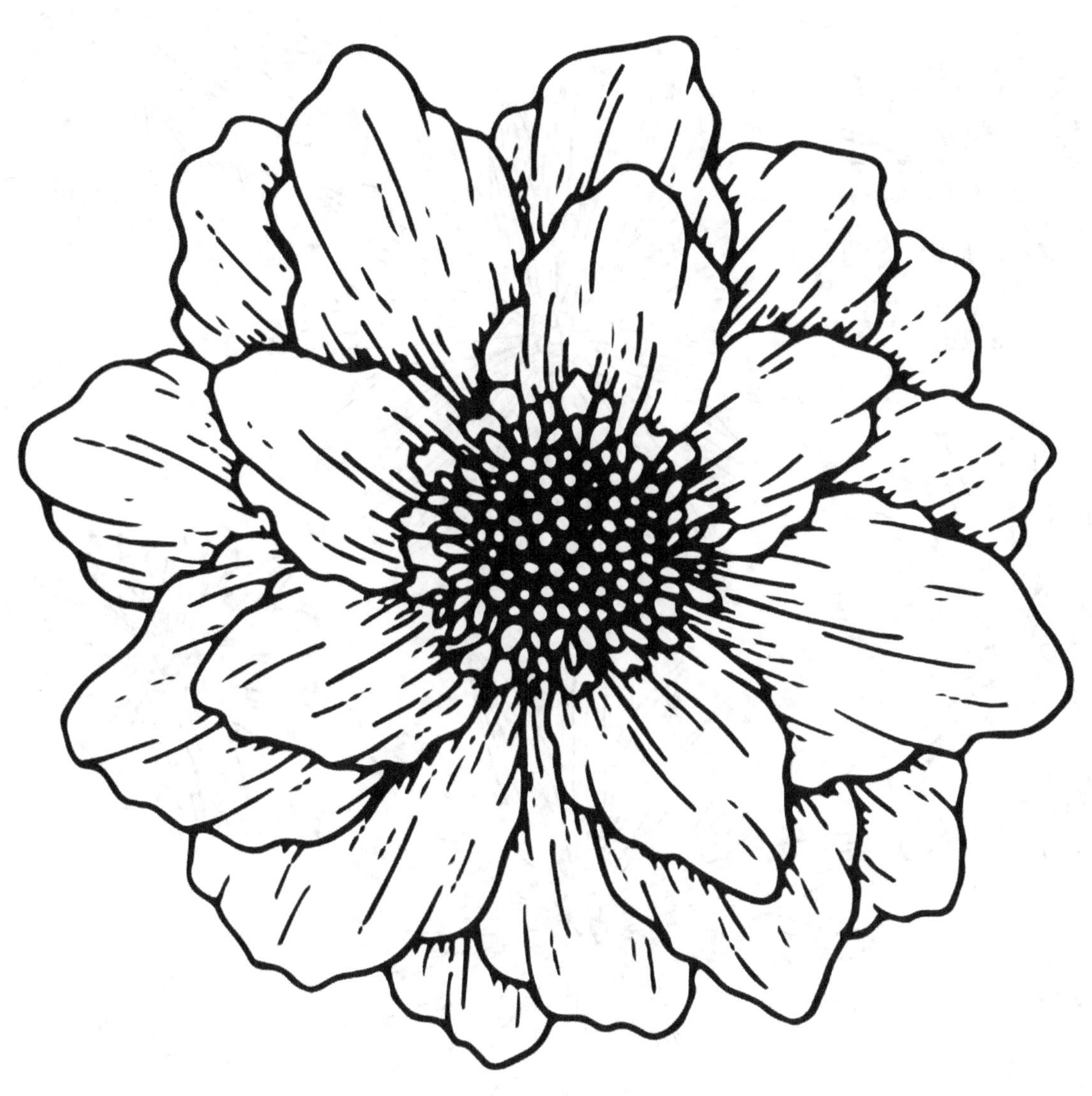

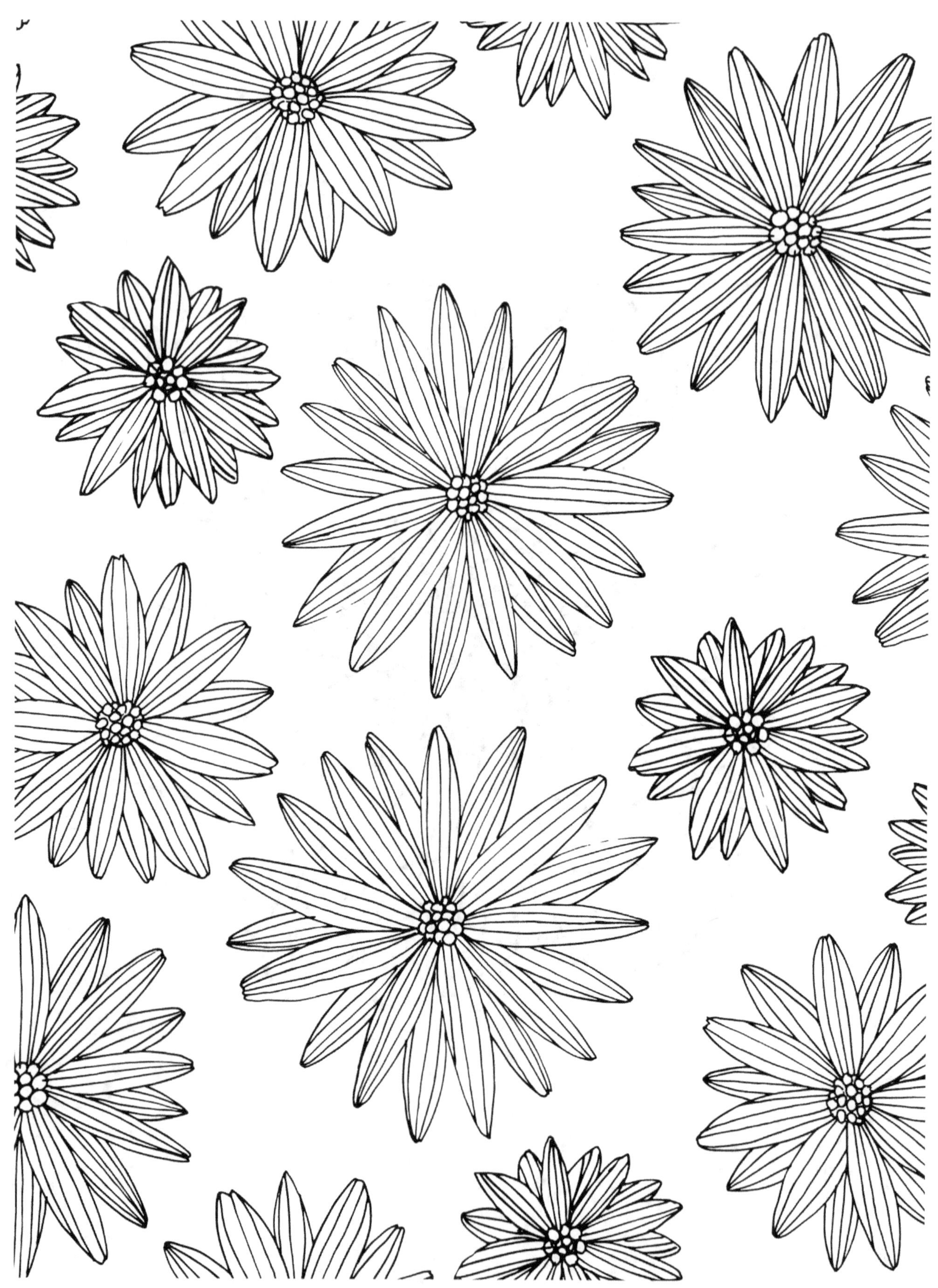

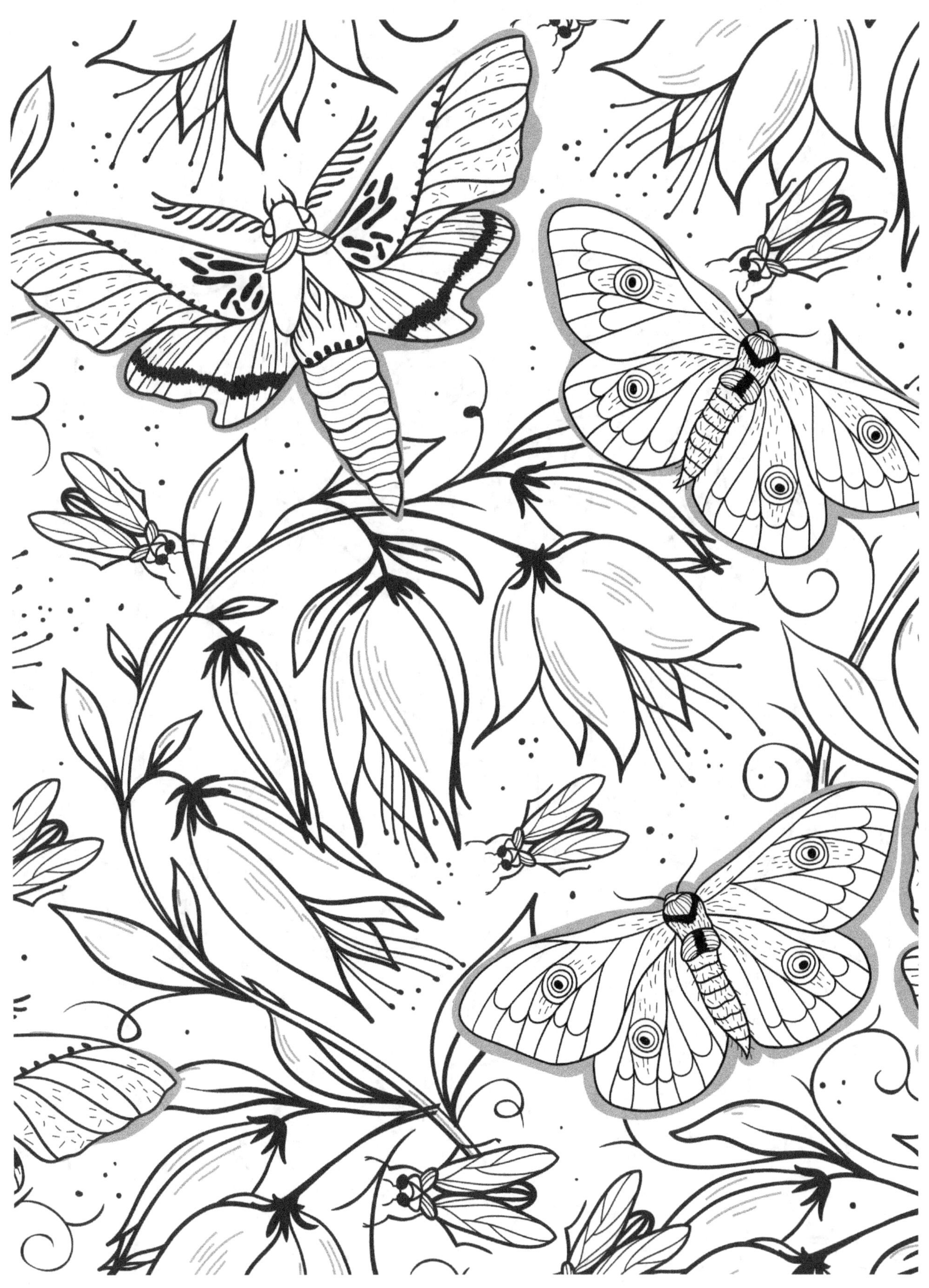

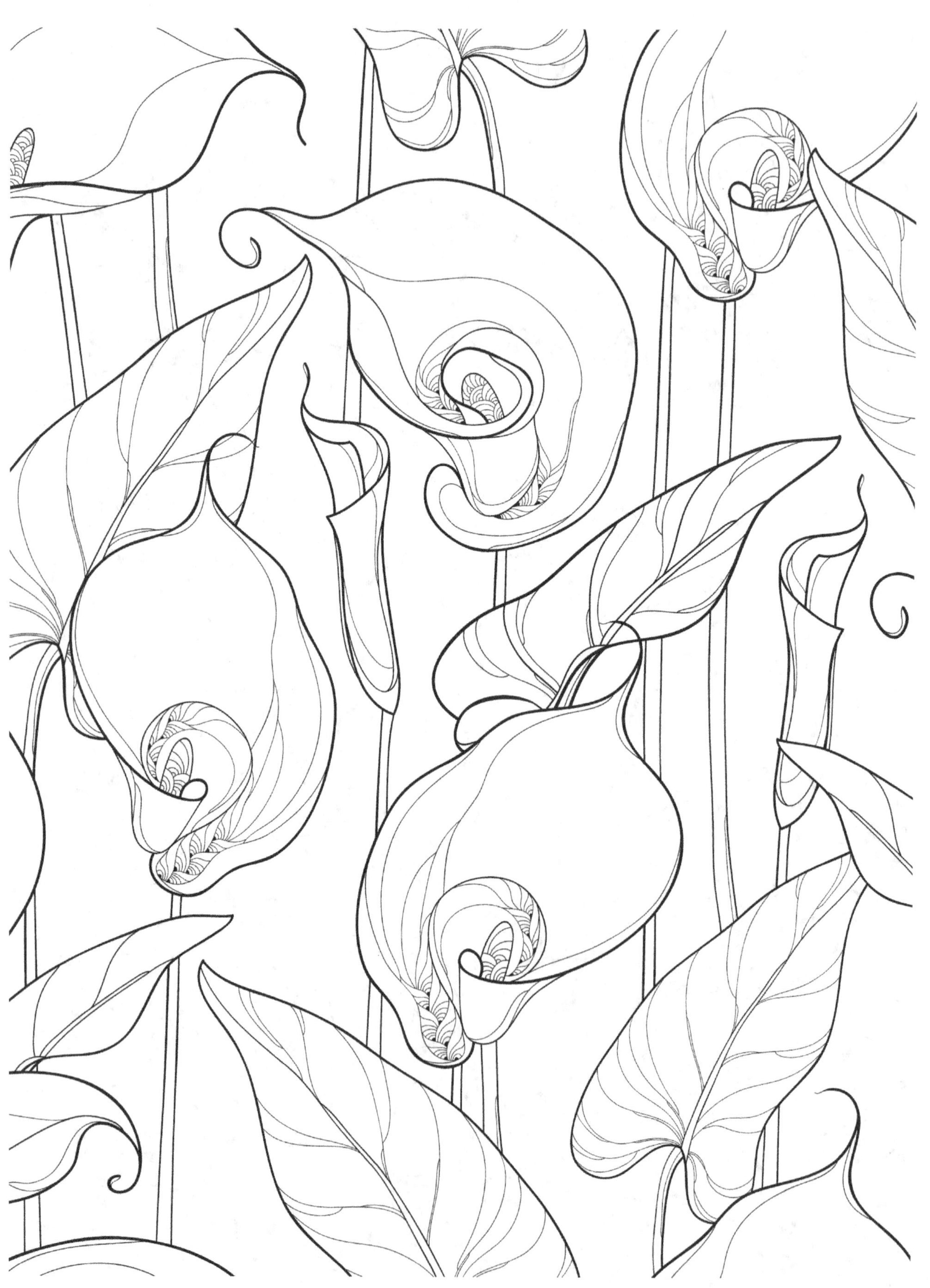

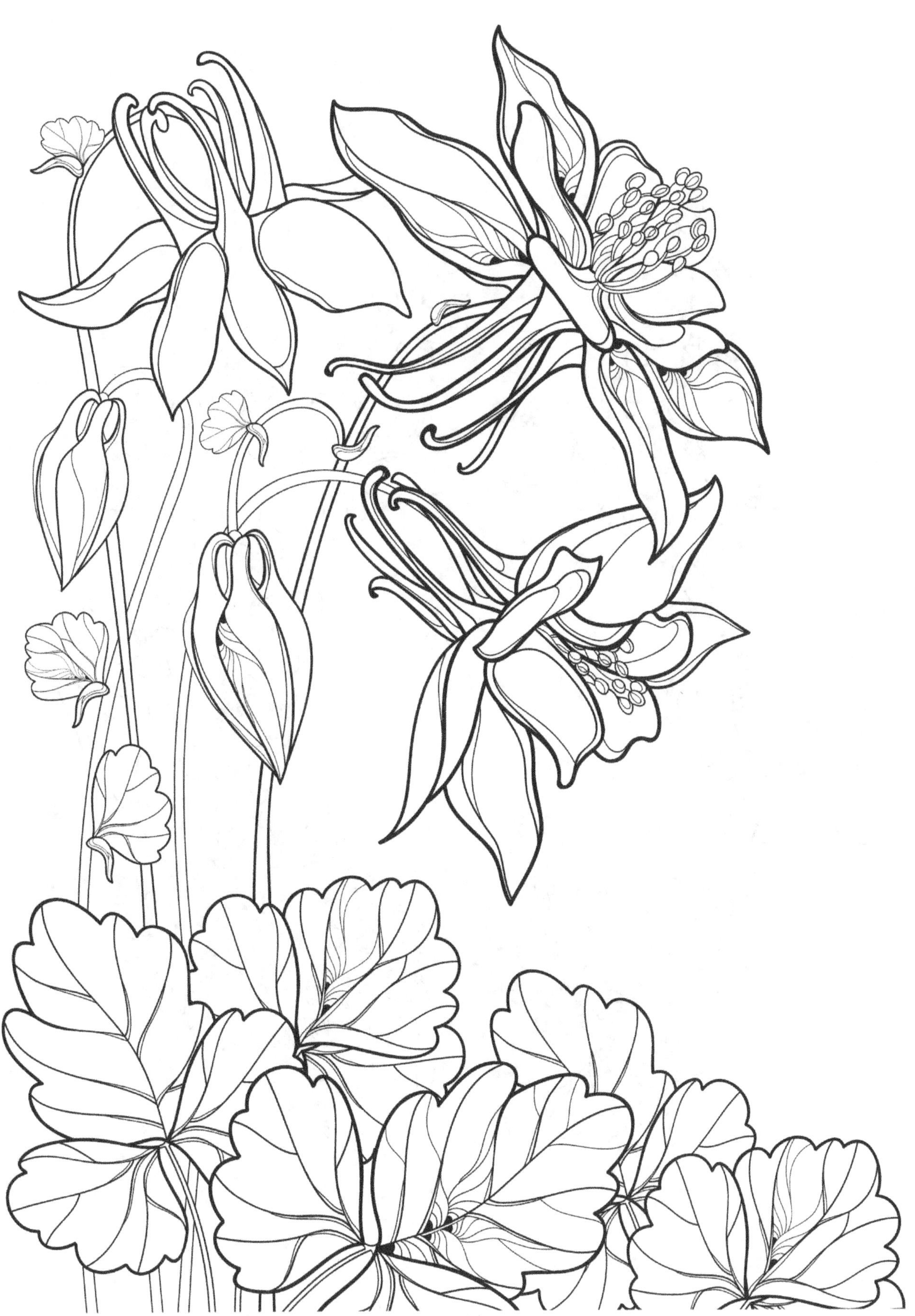

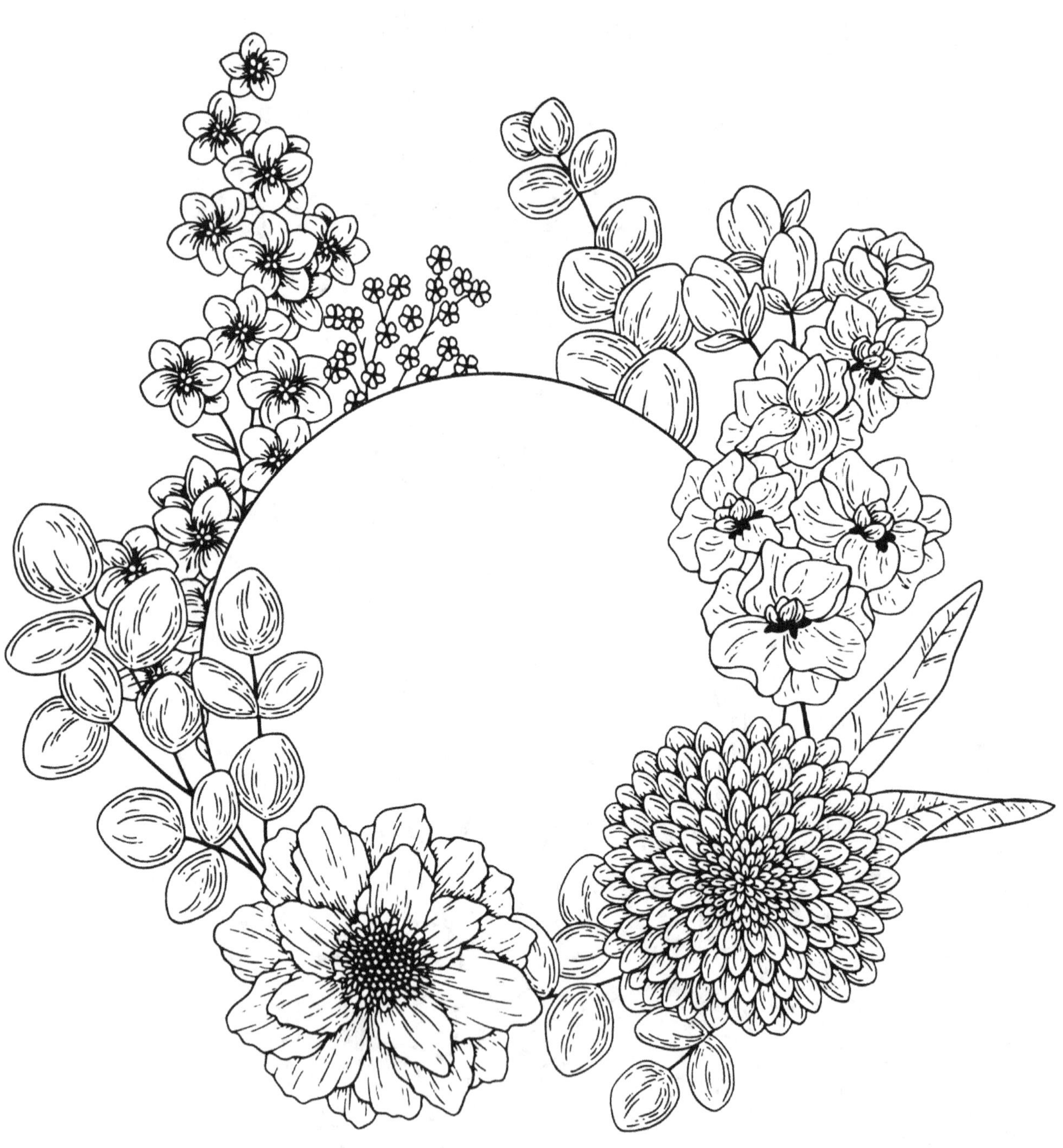

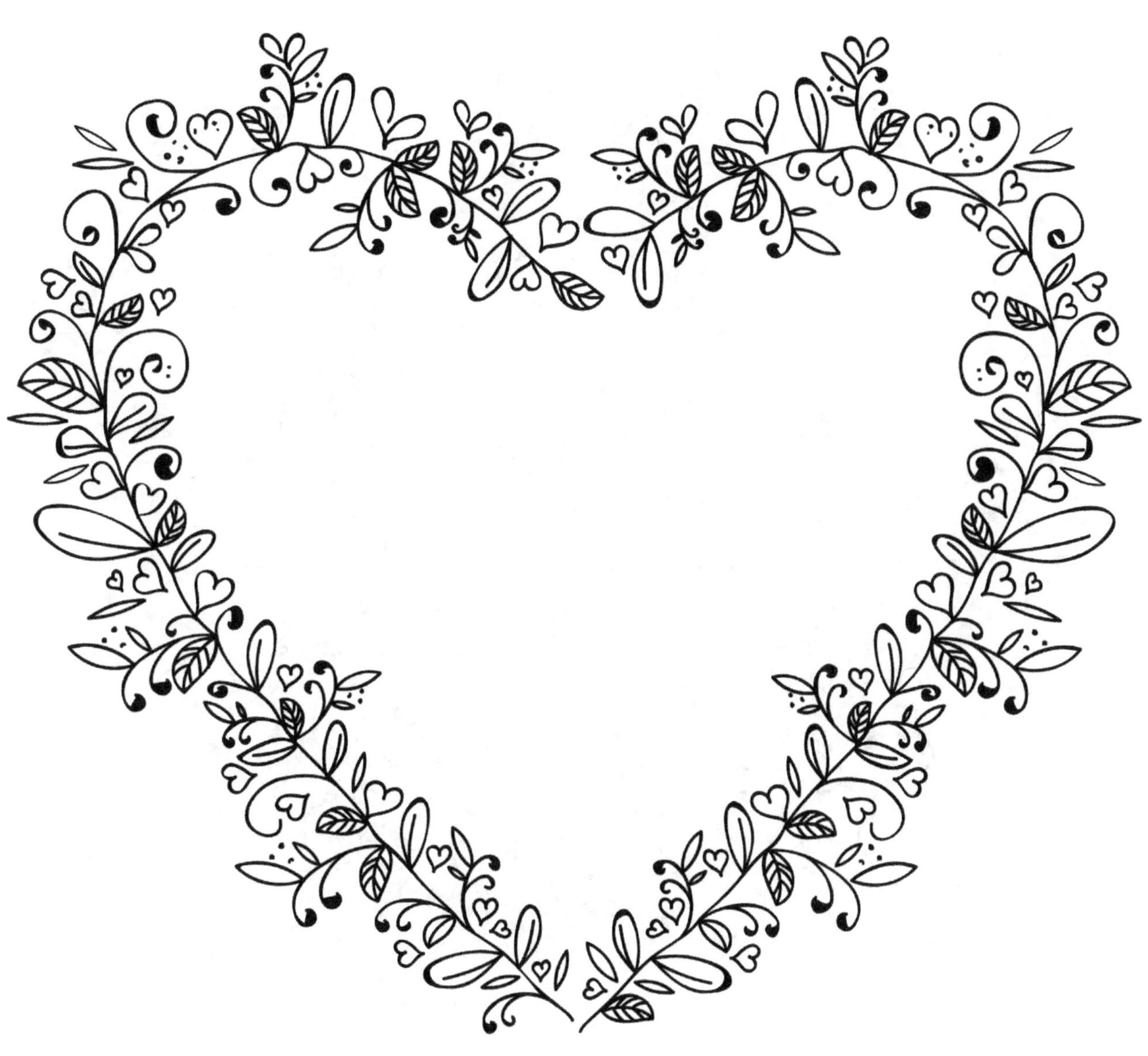

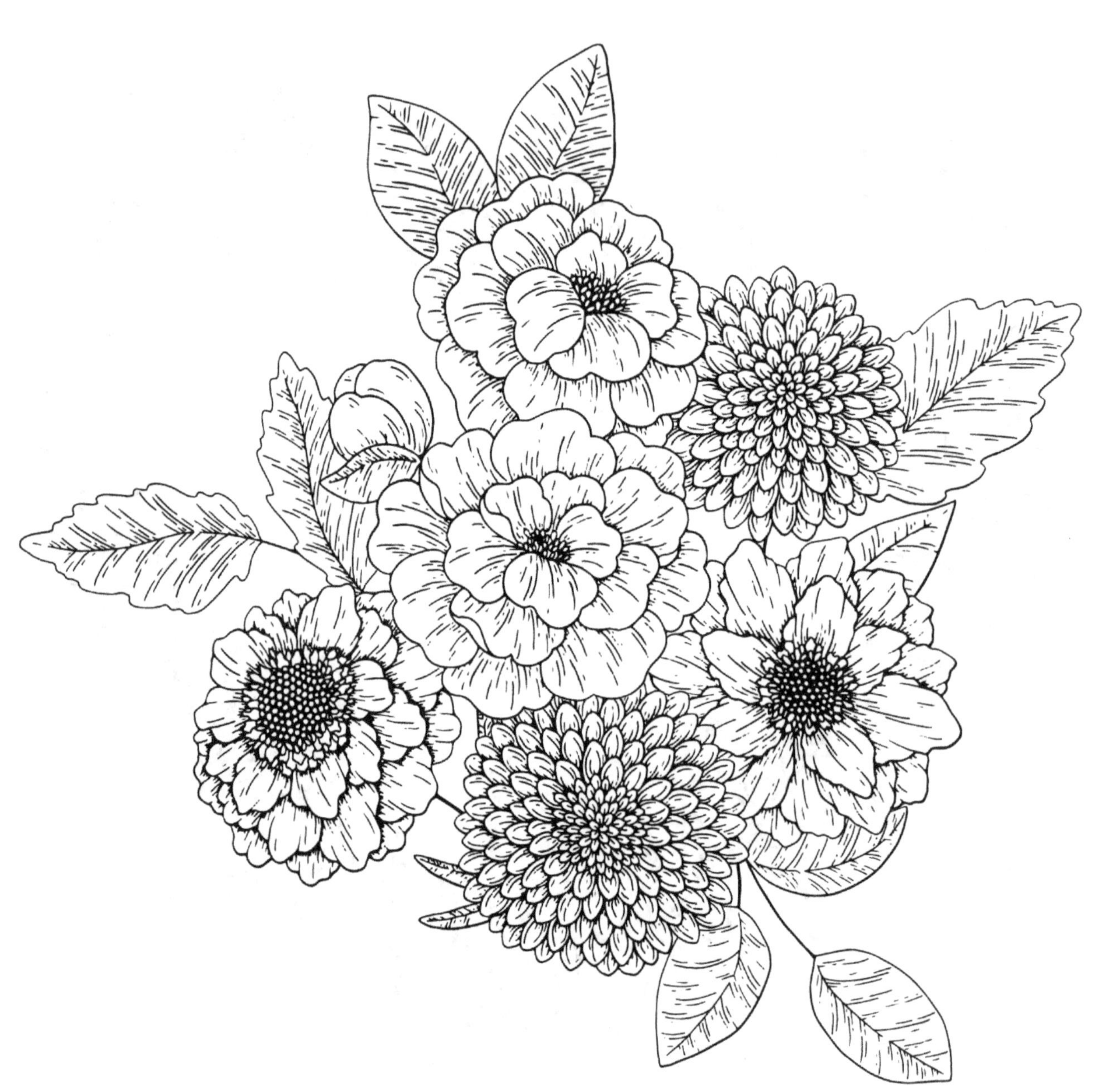

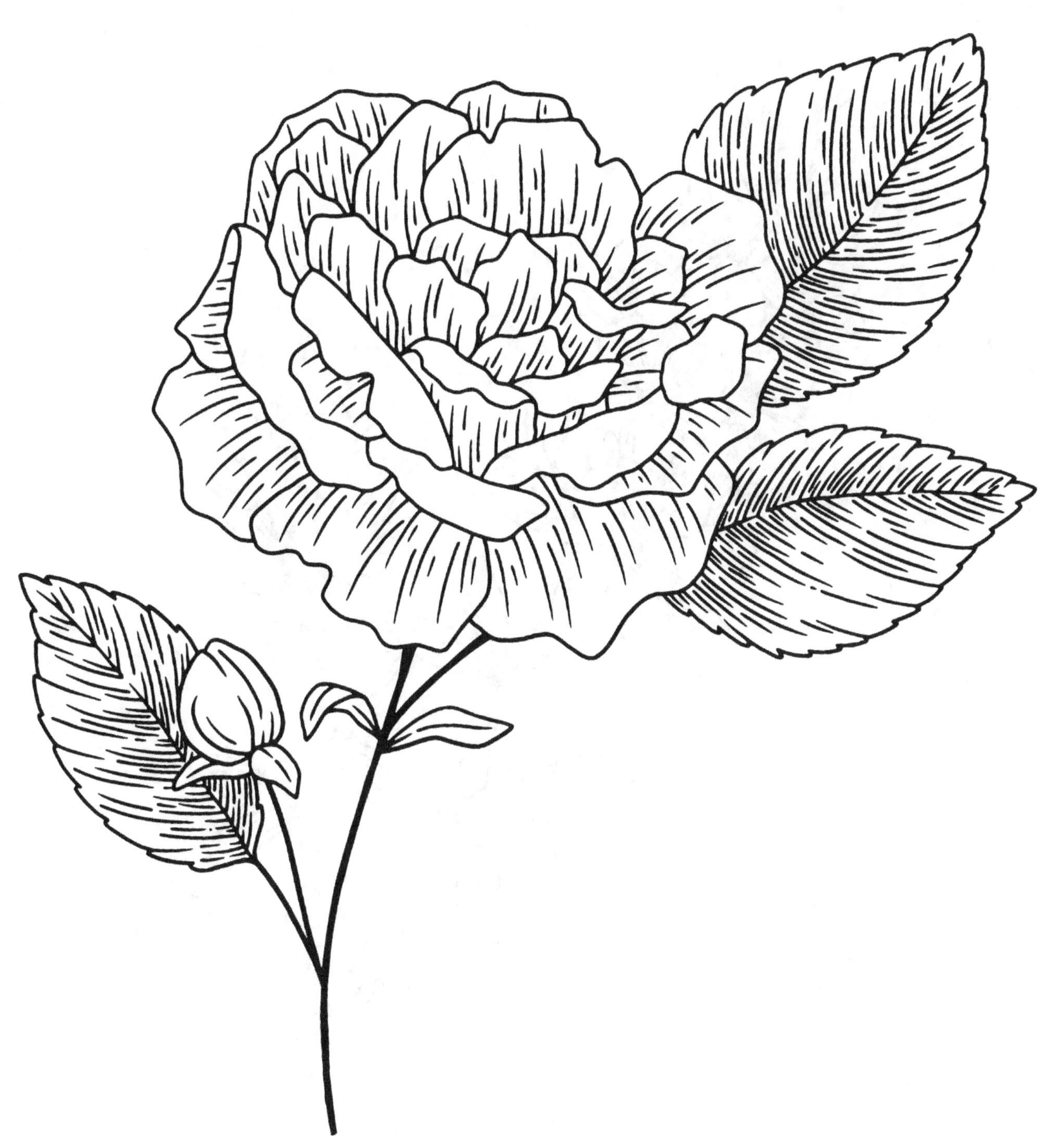

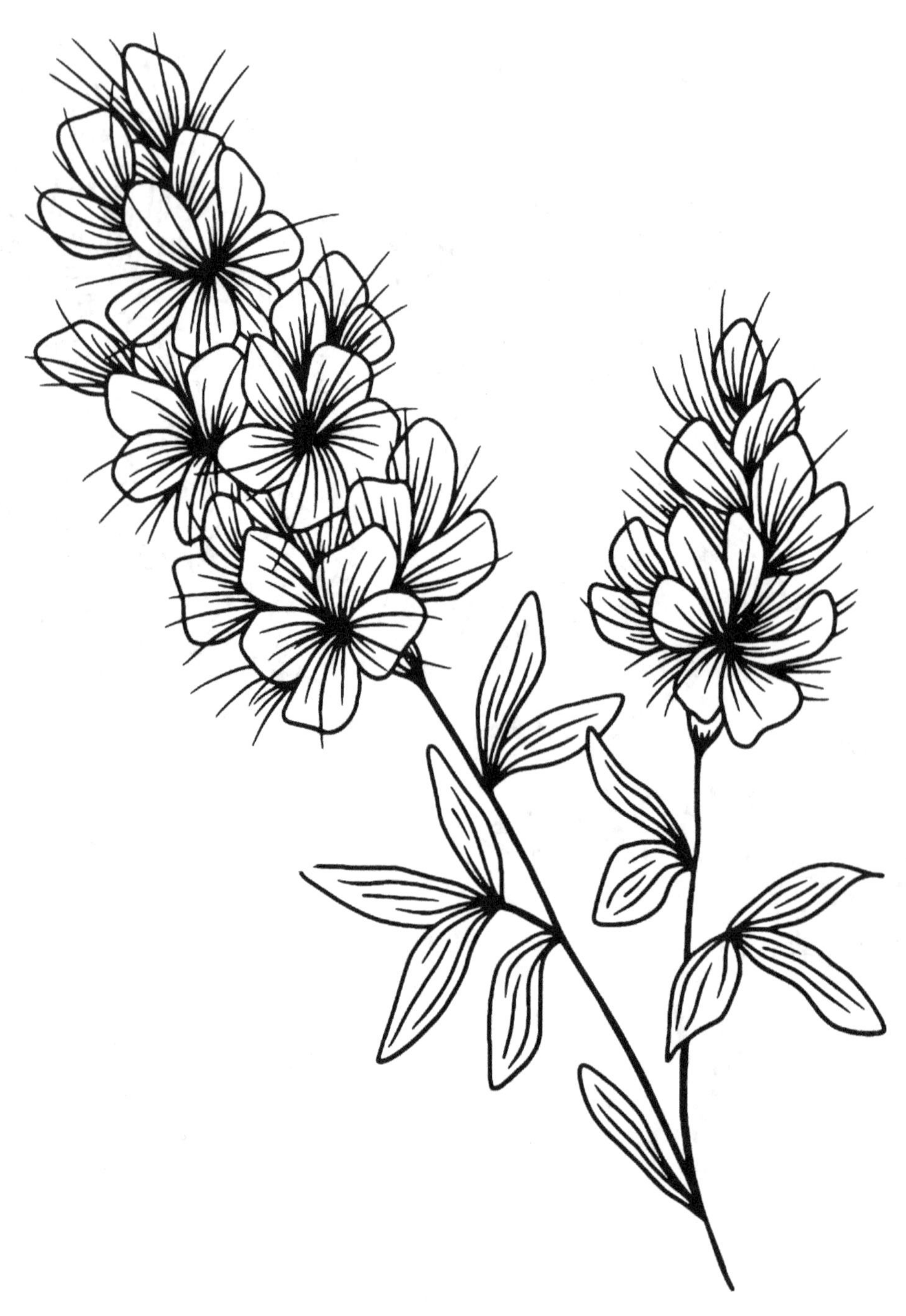

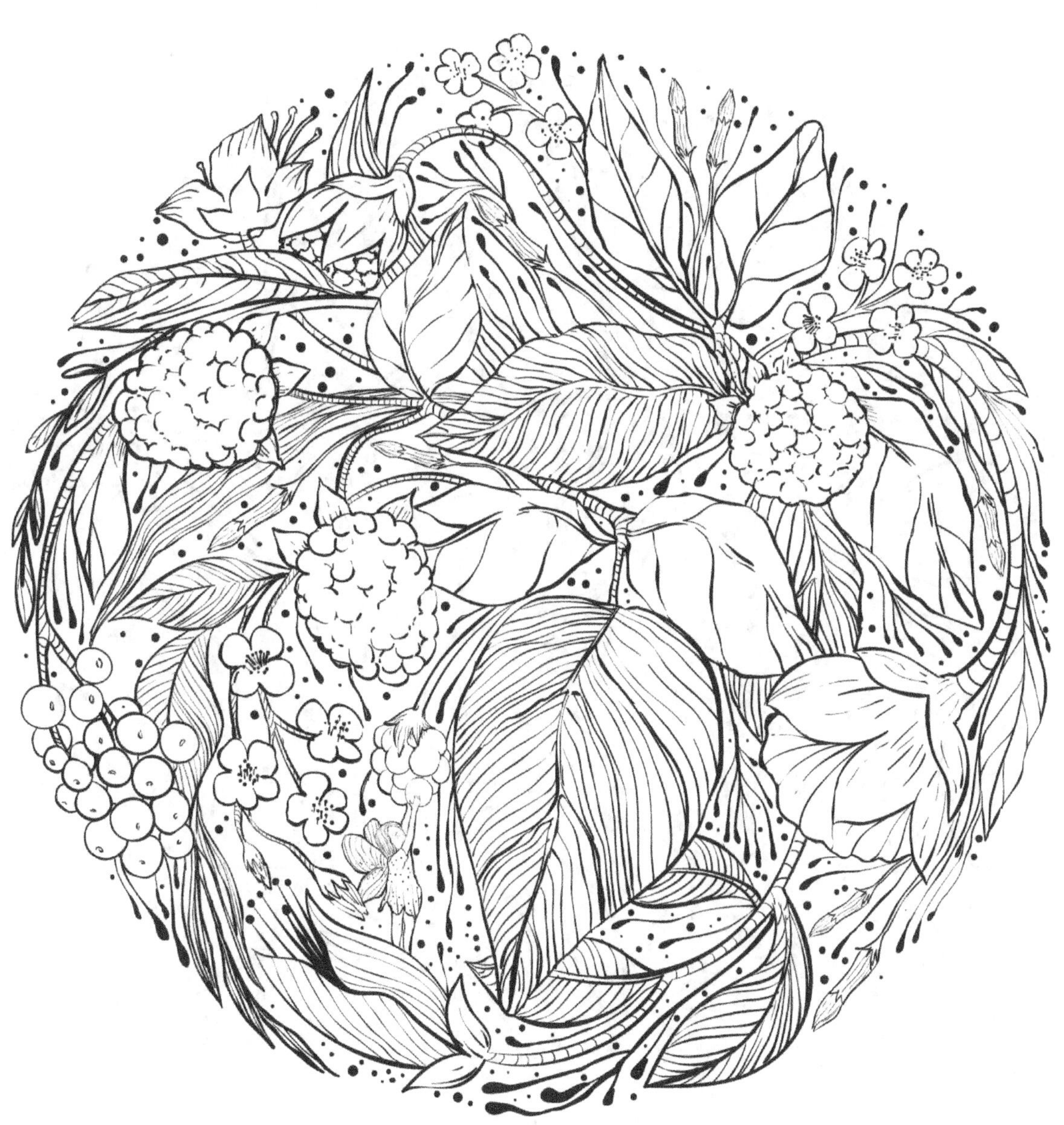

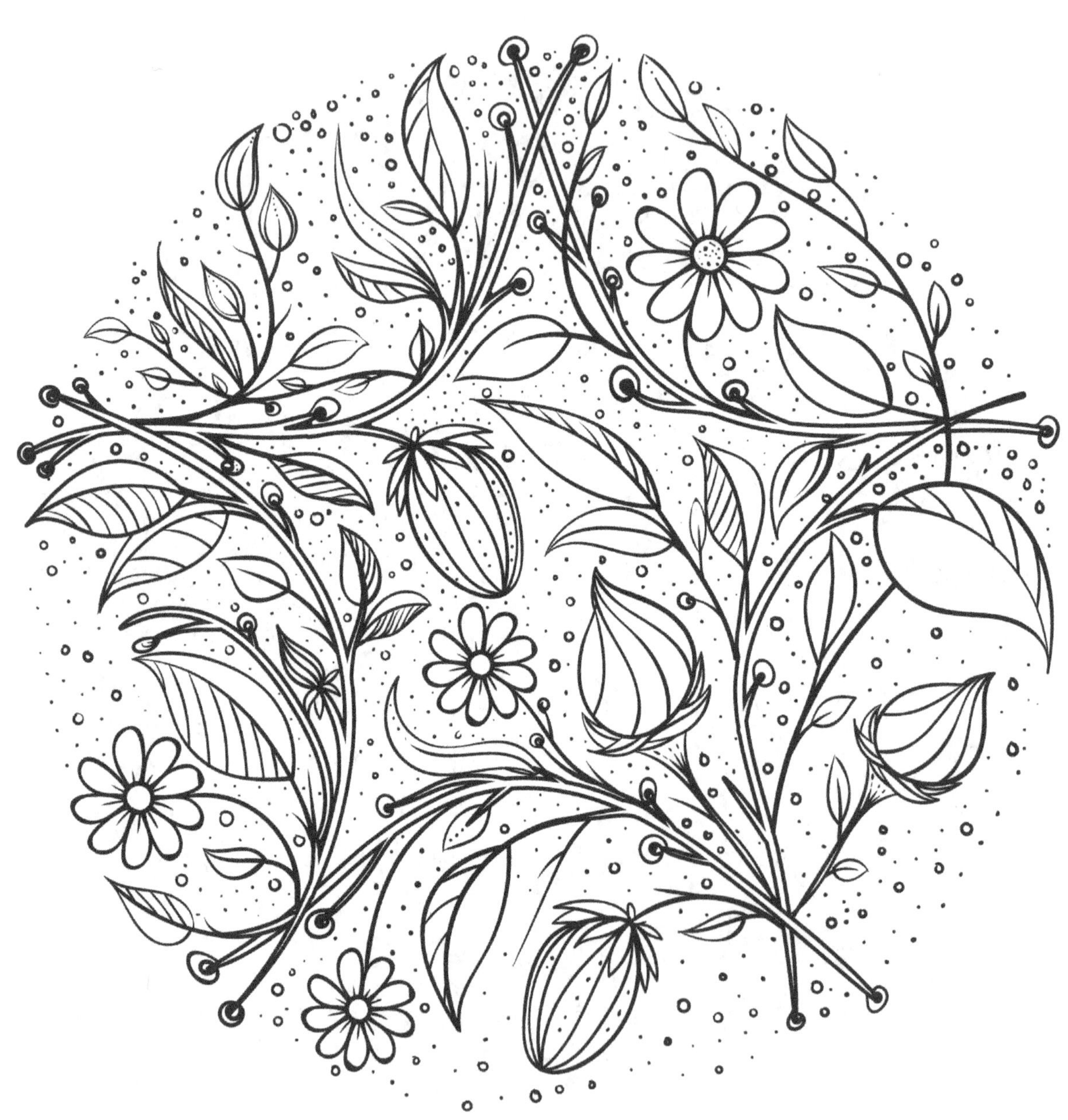

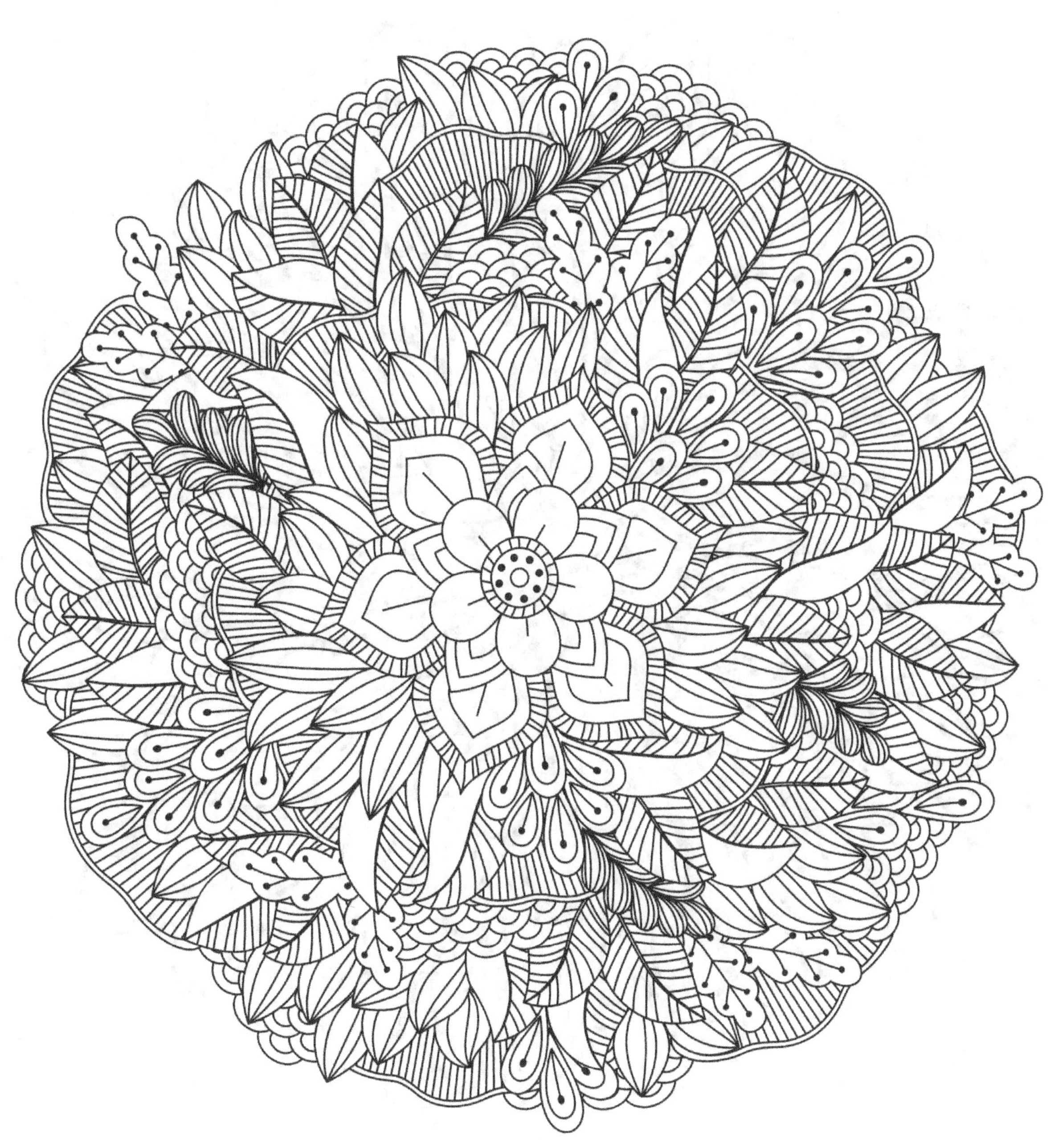

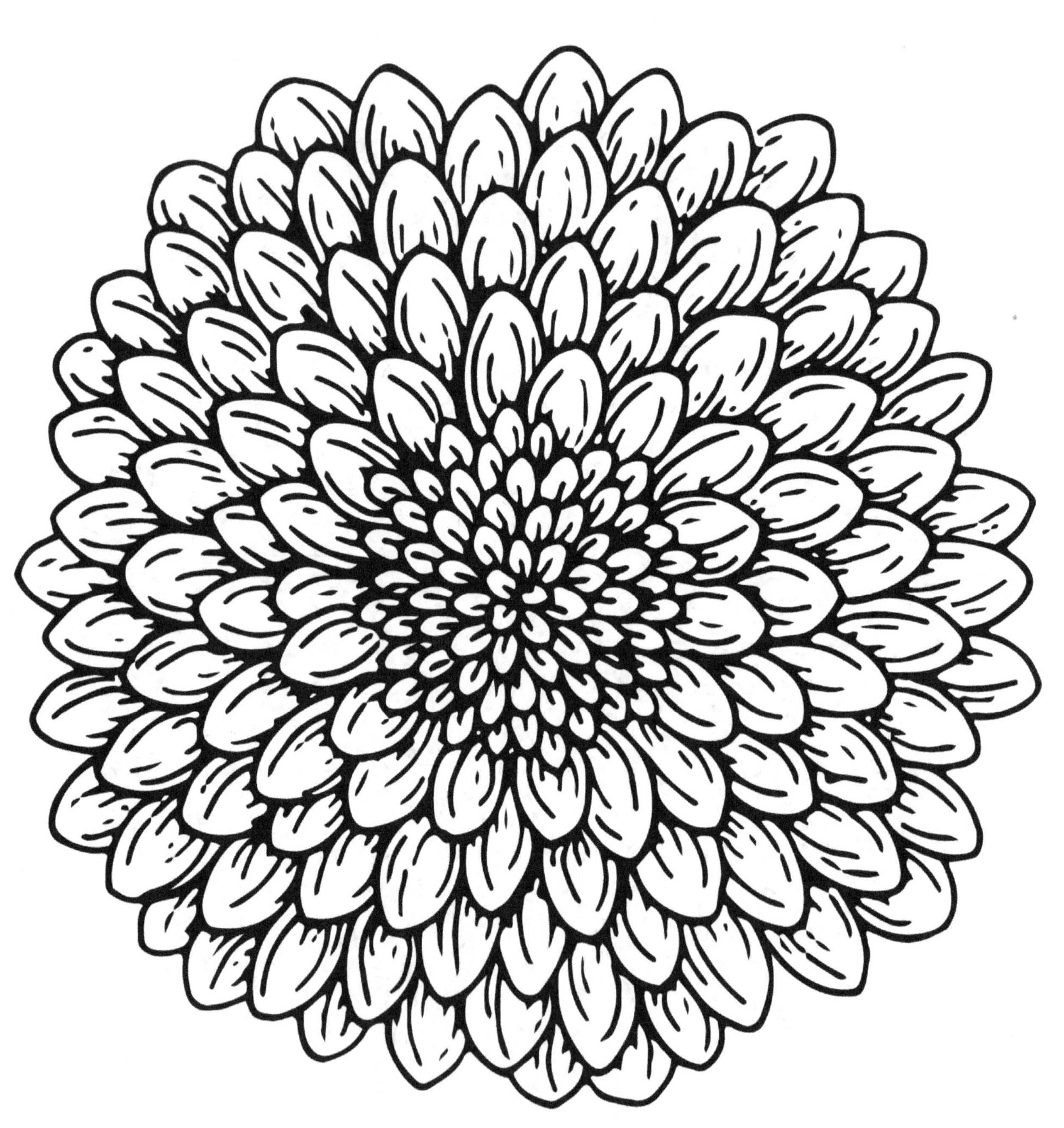

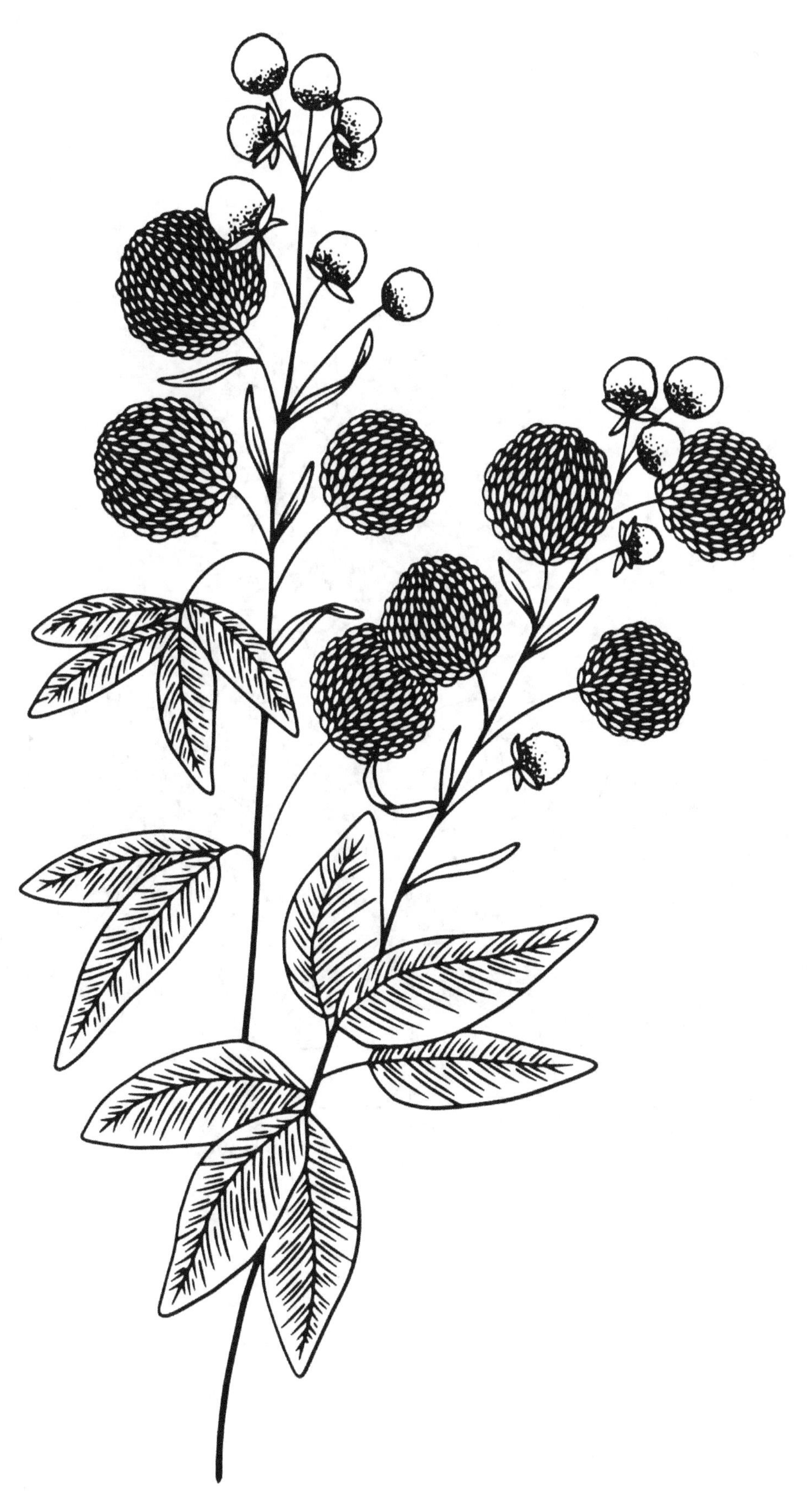

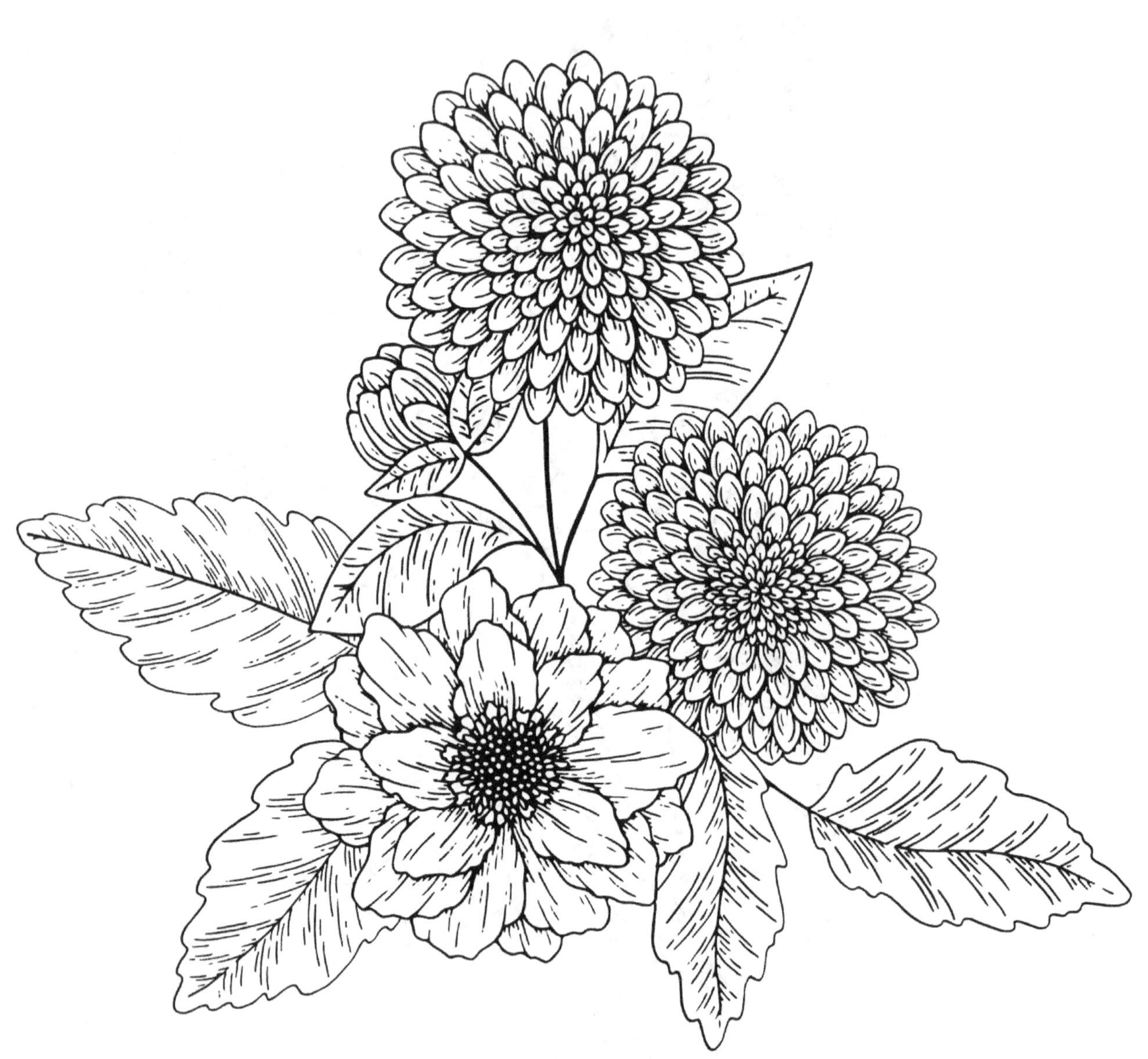